Past and Prospect

Past and Prospect
The Promise of Nazarene History

Stan Ingersol

WIPF & STOCK · Eugene, Oregon

Past and Prospect: The Promise of Nazarene History

Point Loma Press Series

Copyright 2014 Wipf and Stock Publishers. All rights reserved. Except for brief quotations in critical publications or reviews, no part of this book may be reproduced in any manner without prior written permission from the publisher. Write: Permissions, Wipf and Stock Publishers, 199 W. 8th Ave., Suite 3, Eugene, OR 97401.

Point Loma Press
3900 Lomaland Dr.
San Diego, CA 92106

Wipf and Stock Publishers
199 W. 8th Ave., Suite 3
Eugene, OR 97401

www.pointloma.edu/pointlomapress

www.wipfandstock.com

ISBN: 978-1-62564-789-4

Three chapters of this book were published originally in the *Wesleyan Theological Journal* and are used here with permission. Each has been updated, and the article on baptism was expanded substantially.

"Christian Baptism and the Early Nazarenes" appeared in Wesleyan Theological Journal, Volume 27 (1992), 161–180.

"Nazarene Odyssey and the Hinges of Internationalization" appeared originally in Wesleyan Theological Journal, Volume 38, No. 1 (Spring 2003), 66–82.

"Strange Bedfellows: The Nazarenes and Fundamentalism" appeared in Wesleyan Theological Journal, Volume 40, No. 2 (Fall 2005), 123–141.

Table of Contents

	Foreword	ix
1.	The Trajectory of Nazarene History	1
2.	Christian Baptism and the Early Nazarenes: *The Sources that Shaped a Pluralistic Baptismal Tradition*	21
3.	Ministering to the Body, Not Just the Spirit: *Stages of Nazarene Social Ministry*	47
4.	Strange Bedfellows: *Nazarenes and Fundamentalism*	67
5.	Nazarene Odyssey and the Hinges of Internationalization	85
6.	Past and Prospect	101

Foreword for Point Loma Press Series

Point Loma Press was founded in 1992 to provide a publishing outlet for faculty and to serve the distinct theological mission of Point Loma Nazarene University (San Diego, CA). Over time the press has grown to publish authors from a wider range of institutional backgrounds, but its core mission remains the same: to encourage and extend a distinctly Wesleyan theological perspective on various topics and issues for the church today. Most Point Loma Press books are theological in scope, though many are quite practical in their focus, and some address non-theological topics but from a Wesleyan theological perspective. All Point Loma Press books are written with a broad audience in mind, intended to contribute effectively to contemporary scholarship while also being accessible to pastors, laypersons, and students alike. Our hope is that our new collaboration with Wipf & Stock Publishers will continue to allow us to expand our audience for the important topics and perspective of our work.

Point Loma Press welcomes any submissions that meet these criteria. Inquiries should be directed to PointLomaPress@pointloma.edu or 619-849-2359. When submitting, please provide rationale for how your work supports the mission of the Point Loma Nazarene University Wesleyan Center to articulate distinctly Wesleyan themes and trajectories.

Foreword

The Church of the Nazarene experience has always been variegated, culturally and theologically. Such was the natural outcome for a denomination spawned by trans-Atlantic revivalism and created through mergers. American regionalism brought various textures and colors to the early Nazarene mosaic, while the Pentecostal Church of Scotland brought to it certain European sensibilities.

Some variations today seem subtle, such as the "holiness war" that swirled around Point Loma Nazarene University back when the school was known as Nazarene University and located in Pasadena, CA. Local pastor Seth Rees and his followers accused two successive deans of theology, A. J. Ramsey and A. M. Hills, of not being "true holiness men." The accusations missed their marks. Neither Ramsey nor Hills was thoroughly Wesleyan in his particular incarnation of "holiness theology," but neither was Rees, whose background was Quaker. At least theologically, all three were "true holiness men" but of different varieties, taking different mediating positions between Wesleyan holiness and the Oberlin, Keswick, and Quaker holiness traditions. H. Orton Wiley, who initially aligned himself with Rees, later became the very epitome of the Wesleyan holiness theologian.

The Rees controversy illuminated other dimensions of early Nazarene variation. Rees opened up an early version of the "worship wars" when he leveled stern criticisms against fellow pastors C. E. Cornell (Los Angeles First Church) and A. O. Hendricks (Pasadena First Church). Rees believed that authentic worship involved physical and emotional demonstrations and he condemned their churches as "dead," while boasting that his congregation (University Church in Pasadena) "has revival 52 weeks of the year."

Rees also believed that the Holy Ghost could have free rein only in a "Pentecostal church" with a loosely structured polity. He chafed at the Methodist polity that Bresee had enshrined in the Church of the Nazarene and believed it to be a burdensome ecclesiasticism. His complaint reechoed in the 1950s and 1960s by others who left the Church of the Nazarene at that time.

The Rees controversy laid bare many of the underlying tensions in the young Church of the Nazarene. After eighty years of American holiness revivalism, the movement that fostered this revival contained so many prevailing and countervailing currents that their confluence in the early years of the united church led to conflict. With merit, one could argue that later disagreements over polity, holiness, or worship were mere echoes and projections of tensions that initially were present in the Church of the Nazarene at its very beginning.

Timothy Smith expertly used the notion of variation as the heart of his thesis in *Called Unto Holiness* (1962), a landmark study of Nazarene origins. Smith argued that the nineteenth century holiness movement generated "rural" and "urban" holiness traditions within American Christianity. These differed, he said, in temper and mood, with the rural holiness tradition embracing moral legalism, while the urban holiness tradition placed more emphasis on higher education and the individual's personal moral responsibility. Smith advanced the thesis that the marriage of these two traditions occurred at the Second General Assembly at Pilot Point, Texas, and that this marriage gave the early denomination its unique character and provided the grist for its later development. H. Ray Dunning later embraced this understanding in his study of the history of Nazarene ethics.

Today the variations in the Nazarene experience are more obvious than ever before. The Church of the Nazarene is presently organized on six continents and its cultural diversity is greater than at any previous time. Though the church originated on American soil, Americans and Canadians no longer constituted a majority of Nazarenes by 1998. By 2012, they constituted 30 percent of Nazarenes, and some projections indicate that by 2030 the American and Canadian share of Nazarene membership may be at 15 percent. The rise of African Nazarenes to constitute over one quarter of Nazarene membership is one of the key themes of the past quarter century, and it takes its place beside the fact that Latin American and Caribbean Nazarenes constitute an even larger population—currently around 28 percent of total membership.

So in light of these developments, what does it even mean to be a Nazarene?

Past and Prospect examines several dimensions of the Nazarene experience. The book is written from an American perspective, though one that is informed by seven years of living in East Africa. Each chapter has its own focus, but they are united by the themes that have informed my interests and research for a quarter-century.

These interests include, first and foremost, an abiding fascination with religious dissent, particularly in British and American cultures. All religious reform is rooted in dissent. The common thread running through the careers of Martin Luther, Ulrich Zwingli, Michael Sattler, and Thomas Cranmer was their dissent from Roman Catholicism, and yet they initiated different varieties of sixteenth-century Protestantism. John Wesley, life-long Anglican, founded a dissenting movement that influenced eighteenth- and nineteenth-century Britain and altered the very course of American Christianity. The Holiness movement that birthed the Nazarenes was no exception. Movements in religion, like those in politics, typically originate as insurgencies, and the Wesleyan holiness movement began as a conservative insurgency that grew increasingly radical over time. Early Nazarenes dissented from mainline churches, primarily the Methodist Episcopal Church and its southern sister, the M.E.C., South. The numerous women ministers who flocked to the Nazarene standard were dissenters from denominations that did not recognize the authenticity and scriptural validity of their call to preach, nor give them a place to serve. Dissent emerges as a deep, creative, and reforming impulse in religious life when consensus breaks down. The notion of religious dissent is woven through several of these chapters in different ways.

The complex relationship between the Nazarenes and the Methodist Episcopal Church is another theme of this book. I have often heard Nazarenes state that "We are Wesleyans but not Methodists," intended to mean that we are Wesleyan in theology but unlike Methodists in nearly everything else. But historical study does not bear out this distinction. Nazarenes are, in fact, Methodist in church governance and structure, including the offices of general and district superintendent, the General Assembly's binding authority on lower levels of church governance, the General Rules (now Covenant of Christian Character), the trust clause governing church property, and in myriad other ways. I have written on this elsewhere, most notably in an essay titled "Methodism and the Theological Identity of the Church of the Nazarene," and I believe it more accurate to say that "Nazarenes are a believers' church in the Methodist tradition," and then draw the distinction between the particular form of Methodism that Nazarenes enshrine over and against more mainline forms of Methodism, particularly those in the United States and Canada.

Two other themes in this book are related: the Nazarene debts to historic Protestant Pietism and the believers' church style of Christianity.

Both are modes of religious reform, but one is a spiritual style and the other an ecclesial style. They do not have to be married together, and often aren't, but Nazarenes, in fact, have done so. Believers' churches seek to reform Christianity through intentional churches that emphasize a covenant, practice discipline against erring members and clergy, and make a profession of faith a prerequisite for membership. They emphasize Christian comradeship and show an affinity with the poor. Pietists approach church reform through a shared spiritual style and vocabulary that emphasizes justification by faith, testimony, earnest prayer, faithful witness, and missions. They talk about sanctification and the sanctified life; sometimes, they do so relentlessly. With good reason, Pietism is sometimes called "the religion of the heart." Since the seventeenth century, "church pietists" have formed discipleship groups within established or mainline Protestant churches. The early Methodists and their relationship to the Church of England is a fine example of this. "Radical pietists" may attend churches but join no church at all, for they suspect that all groups are morally compromised. "Believers' church pietists" bring Pietist spirituality into the believers' church tradition.

The Church of the Nazarene is located in the latter category, along with its closest kin—the Free Methodist Church and the Wesleyan Church. These denominations are linked by common theology and shared roots in American Methodism, but their blend of Pietism and believers' church styles also provide affinities with groups of non-Methodist origin, like the Church of the Brethren, the Brethren in Christ, the Evangelical Covenant Church, the Moravian Church, and most especially with the Church of God (Anderson, Indiana). Mildred Wynkoop introduced her students to the influence that both forces exert upon Nazarene life in her class on "Theological Roots of the Church of the Nazarene," while Melvin Dieter used the two themes to interpret the nineteenth century holiness movement in his standard history of the subject, *The Holiness Revival of the Nineteenth Century*.[1] Dieter's approach drew upon the outlook of his major professors at Temple University: F. Ernest Stoeffler, a leading scholar of American Pietism, and Franklin H. Littell, a specialist in believers' church studies. Through their teaching or writings, all four individuals have influenced my interest in these themes. The significance of the believers' church emerges particularly in the chapter on Christian baptism, while the Pietist theme underlies the chapters on social ministry and the post-World War II response to fundamentalism.

---

[1] Melvin Dieter, *The Holiness Revival of the Nineteenth Century*, 2nd ed. (Scarecrow Press, 1996).

Another theme surfaces repeatedly in these pages: Evangelicalism's uneasy relationship with Fundamentalism. These movements—so closely related historically—are distinguishable. Both have set up quarters in the Nazarene house, resulting in tensions that shaped the denomination throughout its first century. Those tensions continue even today. My thesis regarding Fundamentalism's relationship to the Church of the Nazarene could not be more straightforward: drawing upon a clear understanding of what a movement is, why it originates and how, I argue that Fundamentalism is an alien influence that tries to implant its values primarily by supplanting the chief concerns that gave rise to the denomination originally. It tries, in other words, to change the conversation.

One way that Fundamentalism often deviates from historic Evangelicalism is in its attitude toward social ministry. Since the eighteenth century, Evangelicals have demonstrated an affinity for ministry to the poor. This was especially true for early Methodists, who ministered to prisoners, rode with the condemned on their way to the gallows, established charity schools to educate the poor, and served society in many other ways. The social implications of the gospel seemed clear to Evangelical abolitionists like the English statesman William Wilberforce, American revivalist Charles Finney, and Wesleyan Methodist founder Orange Scott. Social ministries and ministries oriented to the needs of the urban poor defined the careers of Free Methodist founder B. T. Roberts, Nazarene leader Phineas Bresee, and, supremely, those of William and Catherine Booth, the founders of the Salvation Army. Fundamentalists, though, have often denigrated social ministry and mischaracterized it as a wispy substitute for the "real Gospel." Despite the Church of the Nazarene's twentieth-century flirtation with Fundamentalism, the denigration of social ministries is neither the Wesleyan way nor the Nazarene way. For a time, the Church of the Nazarene even had a General Board of Social Welfare, and this book emphasizes the continuity of social ministry in Nazarene life from the beginning down to today.

The common denominator running through these chapters is the prospect of discovering a usable past. Whether the topic is Christian baptism or Fundamentalism, church polity or social ministry, my conviction is that history has something useful to teach us. The past can function as a lens through which we evaluate the present and assess our future prospects. The lead essay, "The Trajectory of Nazarene History," identifies the primary themes running through Nazarene history. Placing those themes within the context of a "trajectory" allows us to better understand the flow of change in Nazarene life over time. The reality of change reappears in virtually every essay that follows: from early pluralism in baptismal theology and practice to the baptistification of Nazarene baptism; from early Nazarene social ministry understood as discipleship (following Jesus) and witness to new challenges posed by the growing priority of missions and the new context of internationalization; from engagement with Fundamentalism to a post-Fundamentalist renaissance following World War II; from missions to internationalization; and to an examination of current issues that arise out of the past.

These chapters were prepared originally for different venues, including sessions of the Wesleyan Theological Society, the Association of Nazarene Sociologists and Researchers, the 1998 Nazarene Compassionate Ministries Conference, and, especially, the 2008 Wiley Lecture Series at Point Loma Nazarene University.

I deeply appreciate the efforts of Mark Mann and staff of the Point Loma Press to bring these essays together for publication.

Chapter 1
The Trajectory of Nazarene History

When Nazarenes celebrated their centennial in 2008, many were aware that Los Angeles First Church of the Nazarene was already 112. Fewer realized that in Brooklyn, the mother church of Mid-Atlantic Nazarenes was a year older, or that the mother church of New England Nazarenes, in Providence, Rhode Island, was already 120. By 1908, there had been seven Nazarene mother churches—six in America, one in Scotland—each at the center of its own network of congregations.

There is nothing unusual about Nazarene churches or districts being older than their denomination. New denominations evolve from the bottom up unless they result from schism. Scores of Methodist societies had been organized on American shores before the Methodist Episcopal Church was officially constituted in 1784. America's first Presbyterian denomination originated when congregations gathered into area synods, and synods agreed many years later to unite under one General Assembly. And so it goes. The Church of the Nazarene was in this vein. It was the product of *polygenesis*, not *monogenesis*, and by 1915 the founders had knit seven smaller but separate denominations into one.[1] America's national motto, "E pluribus unum," could have been their own.

There was, however, an irony in the 2008 centennial, and it lies in the fact that the church marks its centennial from the Second General Assembly in 1908 rather than the First in 1907. The Second General Assembly was deliberately chosen to mark the church anniversary just fifteen years after it occurred. C. B. Jernigan, the primary Southern leader,

---

[1] Those seven denominations were: The Central Evangelical Holiness Association (New England), the Association of Pentecostal Churches of America (Mid-Atlantic States), the New Testament Church of Christ (South and Southwest), the Independent Holiness Church (Southwest), the Church of the Nazarene (Pacific West), the Pentecostal Mission (Southeast), and the Pentecostal Church of Scotland. The united church also included an eighth entity, the Pennsylvania Conference of the Holiness Christian Church, that denomination's mother conference, but not its newer Indiana conference.

had communicated with leaders of the Eastern and Western churches before those two united in Chicago. But the South's per capita income was less than half the national average and the Southern church could ill afford to support a full and representative delegation to the First General Assembly in Chicago. So a small delegation of seven Southerners attended the First General Assembly and earnestly stated the case to church leaders for scheduling another general meeting in the South. The general superintendents agreed that if the poor could not come to the General Assembly, the General Assembly would go to the poor, and it reconvened in Texas the next year, where the Southerners enthusiastically entered the united church.

The decision to set 1908 as the church's anniversary date was made by the Sixth General Assembly, which was dominated by the church's founders.[2] Their decision reflected that generation's merger-minded mentality, and it provides an important clue to understanding their purpose, values, and self-identity.

Vision of the Founders

Every denomination develops a unique trajectory as it moves through space and time. The founders, whose purpose and aims give rise to the new movement, determine the initial arc of that trajectory. But the trajectory changes over time, altered by internal and external forces. So our first task is to examine the denominational trajectory set by Nazarene founders and then look at the leading forces that altered it.

The larger purpose behind the Church of the Nazarene's rise was the systematic and deliberate effort to attain "unity in holiness." The specific aims that supported this purpose were these: (1) preserve John Wesley's religion of the warmed heart by preaching the substance of his spiritual theology; (2) establish a democratic form of Methodism; (3) maintain an apostolic ministry; (4) align the church with the poor through ministry; and (5) embrace a "mission to the world." The larger purpose and the various aims will each be examined in turn.

---

[2] The general superintendents at the Sixth General Assembly (1923) were Hiram F. Reynolds, John Goodwin, and R. T. Williams, who entered the united church from different U.S. regions: East, West, and South, respectively. The committee that urged the 1923 General Assembly to adopt the Second General Assembly as the event upon which to base commemorations of the church's anniversary was C. B. Jernigan, A. B. Riggs, R. B. Mitchum, E. A. Girvin, and George Sharpe, representing the Southwest, East, Southeast, Pacific West and Scotland. See: *Journal of the Sixth General Assembly of the Church of the Nazarene*, pp. 148–49.

Unity in Holiness

"Unity in holiness" had three dimensions: a particular message, particular methods, and a growing conflict that these engendered within mainline Methodism. The pursuit of unity in holiness was rooted in the nineteenth century holiness revival. Two events in the 1830s marked the holiness movement's advent. The first was the founding of a periodical, the *Guide to Christian Perfection*, published in Boston by the Rev. Timothy Merritt, a Methodist minister. The other was the Tuesday Meeting for the Promotion of Holiness, a weekly meeting of earnest women who sought Christian holiness. They convened in the parlor of Mrs. Phoebe Palmer's New York City home. Men eventually asked to join the circle of women, and by 1850 the Tuesday Meeting included leading Methodists like Nathan Bangs, who headed the Methodist publishing house, and several bishops. As a speaker, writer, and editor, Palmer promoted the quest for Christian holiness all along the Eastern seaboard and in the United Kingdom.

Merritt and Palmer were followed by a generation of Methodist preachers who sponsored a National Camp Meeting for the Promotion of Holiness at Vineland, New Jersey, in 1867. It drew over 20,000 people and led to a permanent body, the National Camp Meeting Association for the Promotion of Holiness. The National Camp Meeting Association's heyday was marked by distinct loyalty to the Methodist Episcopal Church. Nevertheless, fracture lines opened between the holiness movement and Methodist officials. Initially the issue concerned methods. The National Camp Meeting Association spawned dozens of holiness associations across America, some organized at the city level, others at the county level, and others at the state level. This growing network of holiness conventions and associations operated outside formal church structures and beyond the influence of Methodist bishops and district superintendents. This independent network became a source of conflict within Methodism. So, too, was the holiness movement's growing reliance on evangelists, many of whom were wholly unaccountable to church discipline.

Then conflict developed over the holiness movement's message. John Wesley's teaching on entire sanctification had enjoyed a privileged place in British Methodism but had never enjoyed the same status in America, in large part because the Methodist enterprise in America was different. America was a vast expanse, and its frontier was constantly being filled with unconverted people. The churches made the conversion of the American people their primary responsibility. The Methodists excelled at seeking out the unconverted. And they preached far more sparingly on entire sanctification than Methodists preachers did in England.

Timothy Merritt and Phoebe Palmer intended to bring Wesley's teaching on entire sanctification into the center of American Methodist life, but some American preachers thought they were introducing new doctrines, while others thought that the holiness movement lacked Wesley's profound understanding of how the psychology of Christian experience interfaced with entire sanctification. Then, in the 1880s, a new wave of critics arose who disagreed theologically with Wesley and the holiness movement. Bishop Atticus Haygood of Georgia represented believers whose Augustinian pessimism convinced them that entire sanctification was an impossible fiction.

The Wesleyan holiness movement splintered in its third generation. Further fractures developed over the leadership of women, divine healing, the various theories of Christ's Second Coming, and conflicting ideas about the church's nature and structure. Local schisms began in the 1880s and accelerated in the 1890s. By 1900, the Wesleyan holiness landscape looked like this: a majority of holiness advocates remained within the Methodist churches, where they created their own colleges, like Asbury and Taylor, and maintained an extensive network of local camp meetings; while a sizable minority of Wesleyan holiness people were now scattered in over a score of relatively new, small, and different denominations. The groups that created the present-day Church of the Nazarene formed against this backdrop of growing sectarian division.[3]

So "unity in holiness" had several dimensions to the Nazarene founders. First, it meant uniting those who were in agreement on the message and methods of the Wesleyan holiness revival. Second, it meant gathering those who were tired of controversy and sought a peaceful, harmonious life free from the apologetic/polemical context that enveloped Wesleyan holiness folks in mainline Methodism. And, third, it meant healing the holiness movement's own internal divisions by uniting as many factions as possible. The founders consciously sought to create a holiness church. They liked the dynamic rhythm of the movement mentality, but they

---

[3] The theological dimensions of this narrative are detailed in John L. Peters' classic study, *Christian Perfection and American Methodism* (Nashville, Tenn: Abingdon Press, 1956). The two basic narrative histories of the holiness movement are Charles Edwin Jones, *Perfectionist Persuasion* (1974), and Melvin E. Dieter, *The Holiness Revival of the Nineteenth Century, Second Edition* (1996). It is Dieter who points out that the majority of Wesleyan holiness folks remained Methodists. A recent summary of these major points is also found in the chapter on "The Nineteenth Century Holiness Movement" in Floyd T. Cunningham, Stan Ingersol, Harold E. Raser, and David P. Whitelaw, *Our Watchword and Song: The Centennial History of the Church of the Nazarene* (Kansas City: Beacon Hill Press of Kansas City, 2009), pp. 31–56.

wanted it located within a structured environment. Only a churchly way of life, with sacraments and a book of order, would do.[4]

To achieve unity in holiness, the Nazarene founders had to deal with the side issues that divided different holiness groups. Some groups placed a special emphasis on divine healing. The Nazarene founders agreed that divine healing was possible but affirmed that modern medicine should not be rejected. Some holiness groups insisted that immersions were the only valid baptisms; others held that pouring was the true scriptural mode. The Nazarene founders believed that infant baptism and believer's baptism should both be accommodated, as should all three modes of baptism: sprinkling, pouring, and immersion. Some holiness groups held the premillenialist view of the Second Coming as an article of faith, while many eastern Nazarenes followed Daniel Steele, the celebrated Methodist theologian at Boston University, a strong holiness theologian and also a staunch postmillennialist. The Nazarene founders agreed that millennial theologies should not be defined narrowly and exactly by the church. Bresee leaned toward premillenialism but believed that particular doctrines surrounding the Second Coming of Christ were so highly speculative that they should be preached on carefully and sparingly, and expressed in only the broadest language within articles of faith.[5]

For Nazarene founders, then, unity in holiness meant an end to the holiness wars and the union of the fractured pieces of the holiness movement. The Church of the Nazarene was to create a broad middle ground on issues that divided the holiness people internally.

THE RELIGION OF THE WARMED HEART

The "religion of the warmed heart" was at the center of early Methodist experience. Two particular things marked the rise of Wesleyan Methodism in England. The first was the concern for a vital Christian experience. This was evident in the emphasis that John and Charles Wesley placed on a Christian faith that was personal, the importance they attached to the quest for Christian perfection or holiness, and their commitment to

---

[4] The founders' emphasis on "a churchly way of life" is well documented in chapter two. Also see Stan Ingersol, "Methodism and the Theological Identity of the Church of the Nazarene," *Methodist History*, 43 (Oct. 2004), pp. 17–32.
[5] The American Holiness Movement was home to a variety of different millennial views, and each, seemingly, had its own representatives in the Church of the Nazarene. Harold E. Raser surveyed these in "Views of Last Things in the American Holiness Movement" in H. Ray Dunning, ed., *The Second Coming: A Wesleyan Approach to the Doctrine of Last Things* (Kansas City: Beacon Hill Press of Kansas City, 1995), pp. 161–185. E. A. Girvin summarized Bresee's eschatology in his book *Phineas F. Bresee: A Prince in Israel* (Kansas City: Pentecostal Nazarene Publishing House, 1916), pp. 386–87.

the class meeting as the place where saints were held accountable for their progress in the faith.

The Nazarene founders regarded themselves as true heirs of the Wesleys. In contrast to the Articles of Religion in American Methodism, their Articles of Faith were not simply edited versions of the Church of England's Thirty-Nine Articles. Instead, the Nazarene articles emphasized the core doctrine and themes of John Wesley's actual preaching, including the justification of sinners by grace through faith, the sanctification of sinners likewise by grace through faith, the entire sanctification of believers, and the witness of the Holy Spirit to these works of God in human life.[6] And these themes were likewise at the core of their preaching.

Phoebe Palmer and John Wesley nourished the "religion of the heart" in American and British Methodism.

Some of the founders carried on a lingering love affair with old Methodist forms. Following Phoebe Palmer's lead, Bresee instituted a Tuesday Holiness Meeting at Los Angeles First Church that continued until after his death. The religion of the heart was evident in the altar rail's use for prayer in worship and as a place for seeking divine forgiveness and claiming a deeper Christian life. Testimonies, mid-week prayer meetings, and evangelistic services on Sunday nights were other ways in which Nazarenes promoted basic pietism. A primary expression of the religion of the warmed heart was in Nazarene worship, which emphasized preaching that called for personal decisions and music that uplifted the

---

[6] In the Church of the Nazarene's 2013 *Manual*, these are Articles of Faith VI through X.

people. Nazarene worship had a degree of enthusiasm that reflected the church's origins in the holiness camp meetings of the late nineteenth century. Nazarenes drew freely from older hymns, such as those of Charles Wesley and Isaac Watts, but they also drew upon the nineteenth-century gospel music tradition associated with Ira Sankey in the mass evangelism rallies of D. L. Moody, and from a similar music that was associated with the camp meeting tradition. Joyous music with a theological bent was a characteristic of the early Nazarenes.[7]

A Democratic Methodism

The Church of the Nazarene was one of four denominations formed between 1830 and 1910 as an expression of democratic Methodism. The others were the Methodist Protestant Church (1830), the Wesleyan Methodist Connection (1843), and the Free Methodist Church (1861). In each case, dissent from the nature, scope, and exercise of episcopal authority within the Methodist Episcopal Church was either a main point or a supporting one. Each new denomination enshrined a different vision of democratic Methodism, but all shared the conviction that democratic processes had to moderate and limit episcopal authority in ways that the Methodist Episcopal Church had not yet developed. Methodist Protestants and Wesleyan Methodists did away with episcopacy altogether. Free Methodists and Nazarenes renamed the office to "general superintendent," revised its powers, set term limits, and located it within a system of governance far more democratic than their common mother church.[8]

A simple root conviction guides all Methodist polity. This is the conviction that no specific design for church government is revealed in Holy Writ; therefore, the appropriate forms of church governance can be shaped by "common consent" so long as nothing agreed on violates the Word of God. Wesley came to this very conviction late in life. Bresee stated this explicitly in the western church's first Manual published in 1898. In this equation, *mission* can shape *structure*. These assumptions gave British Methodism a structure *without* bishops and American Methodism

---

[7] A conversation with Art Seamans led me to reflect and enlarge on the aspects of worship. See his book, *In Spirit & in Truth* (San Diego: Limekiln Books, 2006).

[8] Bresee's adoption of the term "general superintendent" had two precedents. First, John Wesley had appointed Francis Asbury and Thomas Coke to be "superintendents" of the Methodist societies in America. Those societies, however, proceeded to organize a new denomination, and shortly thereafter the office of superintendent became that of bishop. Still, by 1840, American Methodist literature commonly referenced bishops as "general superintendents of the church." Bresee's other precedent was the adoption of this term by the Free Methodist Church upon its organization in 1861. Ironically, the Free Methodist Church changed the office's name to "bishop" in 1907.

(laboring in a different social and religious context), a structure *with* bishops. The Nazarene founders fashioned a system of governance that reflected their ideals and fit their mission.

The three merging churches of 1907 and 1908 differed in their forms of governance. The Easterners were congregational in polity, while the Southerners embraced presbyterian features. In the West, Bresee began with a simple organization suitable for a single congregation, but in 1903 embarked on a deliberate effort to multiply the number of congregations and expand the connection, including east of the Mississippi River. To manage the growing number of churches, he instituted, by 1904, an adaptation of Methodist Episcopal polity, complete with districts, district superintendents, a property trust clause, and ordination practices that replicated the system under which he had served the better part of his career. The other two groups essentially gathered around his views of governance, though some Easterners did so with a distinct sense of discomfort.

Democratic Methodism was reflected in the church's extension of full laity rights to women. In most denominations women did not have these and were not elected to church boards or as representatives to regional and general meetings. Each of the merging churches, however, gave women full laity rights—a forward looking step in the democratization of the Methodist tradition.

An Apostolic Ministry

Each of the three merging churches also ordained women to the ministry. The New England churches ordained Anna Hanscomb, founder of the church at Malden, Massachusetts, in 1892. The first women ordained in the South—Mary Lee Cagle and E. J. Sheeks—were ordained in 1899. In the West, Bresee ordained Elsie Wallace of Spokane, Washington, in 1902 and Lucy Knott of Los Angeles in 1903.[9]

Early Nazarenes talked about "woman's right to preach the gospel," but they asserted this on the basis of the New Testament witness, not American democratic culture. Openness to women's voices and gifts was based on a specific concept of *apostolic ministry*. The linkage of *women* and *apostolic ministry* stemmed from various sources, including John Wesley's conviction that every Christian bears the gospel and ministers in his or her

---

[9] These women, and others, are discussed in more detail by Rebecca Laird in *Ordained Women in the Church of the Nazarene: The First Generation* (Kansas City: Nazarene Publishing House, 1993).

way. Thus Grace Murray and Mary Bosanquet were among the lay people whom Wesley permitted to preach.[10]

The nineteenth-century holiness movement developed the concept further. Phoebe Palmer's *Promise of the Father* (1859) grounded women's right to preach in Peter's sermon on Pentecost and his resounding declaration: "This is that spoken of by the prophet Joel: 'In the last days,' says the Lord, 'I will pour out my spirit on all flesh … and your sons and daughters shall prophesy.'" God's Spirit to the church establishes and empowers a gender-inclusive ministry, and one does not deny women their apostolic right to preach without denying the Spirit who calls the church into being. Other writers emphasized other scriptures. Wesleyan Methodist leader Luther Lee emphasized Gal. 3:28 as the basis for women's ministry, as did Salvation Army co-founder Catherine Booth in *Female Ministry: Or, Woman's Right to Preach the Gospel*. The Nazarene founders were steeped in this body of exegetical literature, and their basis for ordaining women drew upon Peter and Paul alike.[11]

Thus, at the Second General Assembly, Bresee asserted that women's right to preach and pursue ordination was safeguarded in the Church of the Nazarene *so long as apostolicity was the hallmark* of the church's ministry. This intention to open wide the doors to women's leadership was celebrated publicly from the first. Lura Horton and Anna Cooley were among the seven ministers ordained in Chicago at the First General Assembly. The next year, at Pilot Point, Texas, Mary Emily Ellyson was ordained by Bresee at the Second General Assembly. Women subsequently assumed a wide variety of ministerial roles in Nazarene life.[12]

---

[10] See Paul Wesley Chilcote, *John Wesley and the Women Preachers of Early Methodism* (Metuchen, N.J.: The Scarecrow Press, 1991) and *She Offered Them Christ: The Legacy of Women Preachers in Early Methodism* (Nashville: Abingdon Press, 1993).

[11] Harold Raser refers to Palmer's theology of female ministry as "sanctified feminism." See Harold E. Raser, *Phoebe Palmer: Her Life and Thought* (Lewiston, N.Y.: The Edwin Mellen Press, 1987), pp. 199–210. Palmer later produced a synopsis of *Promise of the Father* titled, *Tongue of Fire on the Daughters of the Lord*, republished in Thomas C. Oden's *Phoebe Palmer: Selected Writings* (New York: Paulist Press, 1988), pp. 31–56. Works supporting the public ministry and ordination of women by Luther Lee, B. T. Roberts, Catherine Booth, and the Nazarene evangelist Fannie McDowell Hunter were reprinted by Donald W. Dayton in *Holiness Tracts Defending the Ministry of Women* (New York & London: Garland Press, 1985).

[12] J. B. Chapman, "October Gleanings," *Herald of Holiness* (Oct. 15, 1930): 3; and J. B. Chapman, "Dr. Bresee—an Apostolic Leader," *Preacher's Magazine* (Dec. 1938): 2. Also see *Proceedings of the First General Assembly, Pentecostal Church of the Nazarene* (1907), pp. 33–34, and *Proceedings of the Second General Assembly, Pentecostal Church of the Nazarene* (1908), p. 29.

A Heart for the Poor

Earlier it was mentioned that two things distinguished the rise of Wesleyan Methodism in England. The second was early Methodism's identification with the poor. Methodism would have been no more distinguished than dozens of other eighteenth-century English religious societies, and the Methodist chapter in church history would have been reduced to a few sentences, and perhaps a mere footnote, had the Wesleys not taken their ministry to the condemned prisoners awaiting execution, to London's poor, to the dockhands in Bristol, to the miners at Kingswood, and to similar places. Instead it can truly be said that the early Methodists gathered wherever the poor did. And this was the basis of the Wesleyan revival—the thing that caused Methodism to burn with a strong, bright flame during the Wesleys' lifetimes. Wesleyan Methodism established itself as a religion of the plain-folk that was taken to the streets.

The picture was more ambiguous a century later. The Free Methodist schism in American Methodism (1861) was based largely on objection to mainstream Methodism's upward mobility and growing indifference toward the poor. Free Methodist founder B. T. Roberts objected that rich and poor were treated differently, demonstrating neither true Christianity nor true Methodism. So, Free Methodists deliberately planted churches among the poor.

Early Nazarenes shared this interest. In Texas, C. B. Jernigan named his holiness paper *Highways and Hedges* in reference to the poor who were invited to the Lord's banquet table after the well-to-do had spurned it. Jernigan's first congregations in East Texas were planted among poor people. In Arkansas, Mary Lee Cagle preached to the prisoners, black and white alike, in the state penitentiary, while in West Texas she planted churches in a cowboy culture composed largely of rootless and dirt-poor young men. The East Coast Nazarenes worked among immigrant groups, with notable success among the Cape Verdeans. Nazarenes in the upper Midwest reached out to Scandinavian immigrants. West Coast Nazarenes reached out to the inner city poor, the Japanese immigrants working in the orange groves, indigenous and immigrant Mexicans, and Chinese-Americans. Bresee's decision to step aside from a long line of Methodist pastorates was the outgrowth of his strong desire to spend at least a year in ministry to the inner city poor through the Peniel Mission. That year convinced him that the poor needed family-oriented churches more than missions. After he was fired by the Peniel Mission's directors, he could have returned easily to a secure place in the Methodist Church. Instead he joined with others to form an inner-city congregation. The word "Methodist" was included in many of the names proposed for the new congregation, but the name that was accepted—Church of the Nazarene—was offered by Dr. J. P. Widney, who argued that it identified the new congregation with the Jesus who stood in solidarity with the toiling masses.[13]

A Mission to the World

At the time of the mergers, the parent bodies had workers and churches in the United States, Canada, India, Cape Verde, Mexico, and Japan. Hiram F. Reynolds was the outstanding personality behind the promotion and leadership of Nazarene missions. Before the mergers, he was the Eastern parent church's secretary for home and foreign missions. He personally organized the first congregations in Canada and guided the selection and sending of missionaries to other countries. After 1907, he served simultaneously as general superintendent and general missionary secretary, using the district assembly platform to communicate his passion for cross-cultural missions. His cause was strengthened by the merger in 1915 of the Pentecostal Mission, headquartered in Nashville, which was equally mission-minded, and by the rise of the Woman's Missionary Society, whose constitution was approved by the 1919 General Assembly. Missions emerged as a dominant priority in large part because Reynolds was an effective advocate, and because the cause was a significant force in achieving the larger purpose of unity in holiness. The different merging partners had brought different priorities to the united church. By rallying the people to the cause of missions, Reynolds helped to integrate the regional entities into a like-minded church with common priorities. The Nazarene investment in a mission to the world represented a significant step in both the inward journey of Nazarenes toward integration and wholeness as a body, and their outward journey into the world.[14]

The Trajectory Altered

New religious groups inevitably encounter wider social and religious movements that soon exert influences on the denomination's aims and direction. Such forces altered the trajectory set by the Nazarene founders.

---

[13] See *Herald of Holiness* (Jan. 4, 1933), back cover, for an exposition of the church's name and its relation to ministry to the poor. H. Orton Wiley was the *Herald's* editor at this time and may have written the piece.

[14] These points are discussed more fully in chapter five. Also see Cunningham et al., *Our Watchword and Song: The Centennial History of the Church of the Nazarene*, pp. 195–231.

FUNDAMENTALISM

The Nazarene encounter with fundamentalism was such an instance. A conflict between fundamentalists and religious modernists developed in the early twentieth century and sharpened in the 1920s. The fundamentalist/modernist controversy polarized American religion and introduced a "two party system" into American Protestantism. Nazarenes—skeptical of religious skepticism, higher critics of the Bible, and liberal Protestant theologies—generally sided with fundamentalists. There was a "fundamentalist leavening of the holiness movement," to use Paul Bassett's phrase. Responding to the beat of an alien drummer, Nazarenes veered toward the fundamentalist camp along with other Wesleyan and evangelical churches.[15]

To the extent that their life reflected the influence of fundamentalism, Nazarenes began losing the mind and spirit of the holiness movement that had given them birth. The primary challenge a denomination faces when intersected by another broadly popular movement is that leaders of the new movement have their very own agenda; as they encounter other groups, they will supplant a Christian organization's founding vision with a different vision of their own devising. At its very heart, fundamentalism was an attempt to change the theological conversation. Its followers wanted to discuss topics that had never been central in Wesleyan holiness theology. Wesleyans had always embraced a high view of biblical authority and talked about the role of Scripture in leading sinners to salvation, whereas fundamentalists talked about the *inerrancy* of original biblical manuscripts that they had never actually seen, sometimes to the point of turning the subject into a fetish. Early Nazarenes had embraced the view that theories of Christ's second coming were of secondary importance, but fundamentalism ardently embraced dispensational premillenialism as the only biblically-correct view of the subject, considering it a subject of major importance.[16]

Nazarene folk theology grew steeped in the dispensational premillenialism that fueled fundamentalist fervor. The Nazarene *Manual*, and successive editors of *Herald of Holiness*, steadily maintained the broad

---

[15] Paul Merritt Bassett, "The Fundamentalist Leavening of the Holiness Movement, 1914–1940: The Church of the Nazarene—A Case Study," *Wesleyan Theological Journal* 13, no. 1 (1978): 65–91.

[16] See the excellent study of fundamentalism's rise by Ernest Sandeen, *The Roots of Fundamentalism: British and American Millenarianism, 1800–1930* (Chicago: University of Chicago Press, 1970). Also see George M. Marsden's groundbreaking work, *Fundamentalism and American Culture: The Shaping of Twentieth-Century Evangelicalism, 1870–1925* (Oxford: Oxford University Press, 1980).

middle ground that emphasized liberty of conscience on matters regarding the Second Coming. Evangelists and pastors often did not. The evangelist's typical "Second Coming" sermon and popular tracts took a definite point of view regarding "the Rapture" and pre-, post-, and mid-tribulation theories. The acceptance of dispensational premillenialism by some pastors and many lay people opened a gulf between them and the church's theologians. No major Nazarene theologian has ever embraced dispensationalism—not H. Orton Wiley, who was cagey about his eschatology; nor A. M. Hills, an ardent postmillennialist; nor Olive Winchester, an amillenialist; nor any significant Nazarene theologian in the church's second half-century. Part of the suspicion with which some Nazarenes came to regard their church colleges and theological institutions is rooted in the fact that Nazarene theologians have never adopted dispensationalism's pessimism or worldview.

Fundamentalists also adopted a spirit of militancy toward non-fundamentalists. By emphasizing their belief that the "popular churches" were fallen, dispensationalists bred an attitude of disdain for non-evangelical Christians. One result is that churches in which fundamentalists ruled soon lost any semblance of an ecumenical soul.

Fundamentalism sought to change the Church of the Nazarene's mind and redirect its energies. Nazarenes emerged from their fundamentalist phase through groundwork laid by H. Orton Wiley and carried out by a new generation of Nazarene theologians who assumed leadership in the church after World War II, but remnants of the fundamentalist leavening of Nazarene life remain with us today.

The Pull of the Evangelical Mainstream

As it aged, the Church of the Nazarene edged steadily toward the evangelical mainstream. Fundamentalism provided one push but other forces were also at work.

The evangelical mainstream exerts a magnetic pull on the Church of the Nazarene. That mainstream is a constant work-in-progress. Methodists were a key force in shaping nineteenth-century evangelicalism. They possessed an exceedingly small share of the American religious franchise in 1775, but by 1850 they constituted the nation's largest religious bloc and influenced the thinking and methods of other denominations. This changed in the twentieth century. By 1920, the Methodist Episcopal Church had developed a degree of theological pluralism and was no longer regarded as a reliable evangelical ally. Moreover, the surge of Baptist energies made that group a larger and more influential evangelical group by the mid-twentieth century. This was followed by the growth of Pentecostal and charismatic denominations later in the twentieth century. With reason, we can think of the nineteenth century as the Methodist century, and the twentieth century as the Baptist and Pentecostal century.

Although American evangelicalism is in constant motion, it differs in its dynamics from fundamentalism. Evangelicalism is not rooted in dissent, which fuels all genuine movements; instead, it reflects the theologically conservative instincts of churches and individuals who face modernity but are uncomfortable with hard-line fundamentalism on the right and uncritical ecumenism on the left. Instead, evangelicals find themselves connected with one another across theological boundaries based on a shared commitment to orthodox forms of Protestantism. Nazarenes can think of popular evangelicalism as "the water in which we swim."

Churches gravitate toward the evangelical mainstream for many reasons. Often their wild and wooly days are over and they want to conform. They also gravitate toward it because churches can fail at their catechetical tasks and the people—such as Wesleyan people—sometimes can no longer distinguish between the Wesleyan message and the message of radio and television preachers. The evangelical water in which Nazarenes swim has influenced popular Nazarene theology in numerous ways. As Baptists and the Assemblies of God have exerted increasing influence on American evangelicalism, Nazarene baptismal theology has changed. So, believer's baptism predominates today, and immersion is strongly preferred over other modes of baptism. The evangelical mainstream has also reshaped popular eschatology and worship practices. The early Nazarene commitment to women in ministry weathered the fundamentalist years rather well. As late as 1955, over 250 Nazarene churches in the United States had women as their pastors.[17] The sharpest period of decline in women in ministry occurred after this date, as Nazarenes increasingly conformed to the evangelical mainstream.

So the loss of distinctive ideas to a generic evangelicalism is a risk in the Nazarene relationship to wider evangelicalism. There are, however, other aspects of this relationship to consider.

First, the point must be made that the Church of the Nazarene, as a product of the nineteenth-century holiness movement, was born in the cradle of American evangelicalism. One cannot do justice to the story of the Wesleyan holiness movement if it is isolated from the wider story of

---

[17] See Richard W. Houseal, "Women Clergy in the Church of the Nazarene: An Analysis of Change from 1908 to 1995," M.A. thesis, University of Missouri at Kansas City, 1996.

nineteenth-century Evangelicalism. Similarly, one cannot truly understand the Church of the Nazarene's expansion and internationalization apart from the larger story of world evangelization and Christianity's global expansion in the twentieth century.

Second, every denomination influenced by fundamentalism had to move beyond that mindset by devising its own strategies. But the post-fundamentalist era in American evangelicalism also involves shared work across denominational lines. Nazarene theologians like W. T. Purkiser, Kenneth Grider, Mildred Wynkoop, William Greathouse, and others participated in a post-World War II "evangelical renaissance," a movement in evangelical theology that was designed, in the words of E. J. Carnell of Fuller Theological Seminary, to move evangelicals away from "the small talk of the cult" and back to conversation on historic themes. The Nazarene theologians of that era consciously followed the lead of Carl F. H. Henry, Carnell, Timothy Smith, and other evangelicals whose agenda was to create a post-fundamentalist evangelicalism.

William Greathouse (left) and W. T. Purkiser (right) were among the Nazarene theologians who edged the church away from Fundamentalism in conjunction with the post-war Evangelical renaissance.

Evangelicalism underwent a second stage beginning in the late 1960s. Influenced by the Civil Rights movement and the desire for a holistic Gospel that combined social action with evangelism, and by a growing body of theological literature that took seriously the city as a place of Christian ministry, Nazarenes joined other evangelicals in reclaiming ministry in the urban context. Nazarenes did not travel this path alone; they traveled it with other evangelicals. This new phase that emerged more fully in Nazarene life in the 1970s and '80s was part of a wider reorientation of the global evangelical movement. An early manifesto for action was found in the Chicago Declaration of Evangelical Social Concern issued by leading "young evangelicals" in 1973. But its positioning within the broader context of world evangelization was solidified the following year in the Lausanne Covenant, a document growing out of the 1974 International Congress on World Evangelization, which gave the imprimatur of the evangelical establishment to urban and social ministries. This new movement, in which Nazarenes were fellow-travelers, shaped not only new urban and social ministries in American Nazarene life but laid the groundwork for Nazarene Compassionate Ministries International with its global network that utilizes the denomination's regional and district structures.

Nazarene affinity with wider evangelical concerns, then, has had positive and negative consequences alike. It is an ambiguous relationship that has shaped the first century of Nazarene life in various ways.

AMERICAN CULTURE

If evangelicalism is the water in which we swim, American culture is the air that many Nazarenes breathe. This was certainly true for the great majority of twentieth-century Nazarenes. It remains true for the 30 percent of Nazarenes who were Americans in 2013.

American culture was a discernible influence on Nazarene life from the outset. Early on, Americanization was evident in the democratic ethos that shaped Nazarene structures, including the periodic election to set terms for pastors, district superintendents, general superintendents, and other general officers. It was evident in the decision that women were eligible to participate in every sphere of church life and governance, and that laity participate in decision-making at all levels—local, district, and general.

The projection of American culture into the church has had its negative side. For instance, early Nazarenes rarely rose above the racial prejudices of their day. Their attitudes toward African Americans varied widely across the United States, resembling those dominant in a given section at a given time. In the 1920s and '30s, E. C. DeJernett and John Oliver, from Texas and Arkansas, deplored the church's apathy toward African Americans; but apathy still ruled. In 1959, distribution ceased of *The Other Sheep* magazine's Christmas issue; the "controversial" cover depicted a black Holy Family. The original covers were stripped; the new ones showed white teenagers singing carols. The General Assembly began grappling with the implications of basic civil rights as early as 1956, and one of the prophetic voices raised was Olivet's sociologist F. O. Parr, the author of *Perfect Love and Race Hatred* (1964). Throughout the twentieth century,

Nazarene attitudes towards African Americans were largely projections of different strains of national culture into the church's life.[18]

As a human creation, culture is understood theologically as a reflection of the human condition, exhibiting the full range of human traits and aspirations—tragedy and hope, sin and redemption. Significant cultural forces shape our personal and corporate identities: the State, economic life, folkways, the arts. But our fundamental identities as Christians are supposed to be shaped by the Bible, and particularly by what it tells us about Jesus' life and teachings. Yet, as H. Richard Niebuhr demonstrated in a seminal book in 1951, Christians have related Christ and culture variously across the centuries: merging them, holding them in tension, striving to reform culture, or creating counter-cultures.[19] The eternal question for Christians of each generation and place remains: will the church find its life, vision, and values primarily in the Christian Scriptures or draw these instead from the culture in which it moves?

American culture changed dramatically in the twentieth century, though only two features will be noted here: America's rise to global power, and a parallel culture of affluence, both spurred by World War II. Americans believed that theirs was an important nation before that war; afterward, they believed it to be an indispensable one. America's military and economic reach spanned the world. How did this development affect the way that Americans saw themselves, and how did others view them? One interesting assessment appeared in the 1958 novel, *The Ugly American,* in which Americans operating in Asia undermined their own influence and interests through arrogant pride and cultural elitism. But the same book also portrayed a character that came to terms with his limitations and began learning from his Asian associates. Like European

---

[18] Copies of the *Other Sheep* for December 1959 with their original covers are in the Nazarene Archives in the World Mission Collection. See the Church of the Nazarene's *Manual* (1956), pp. 325–26. The resolution on race and discrimination adopted in 1956 was an attempt to respond to issues raised by the civil rights movement and called for recognition of the "sacredness of personality," the incompatibility of racial discrimination with Christian faith, and "the Christian goal of full participation by all in the life of the community." However, these statements were broad enough that even segregationists could affirm them from their own angle of vision. An attempt in 1964 to urge that Nazarene citizens support civil rights legislation in local, state, and national government was deftly turned aside, and the General Assembly affirmed the need for "peaceful action" and the belief that "the real solution for misunderstanding between racial groups will come when the hearts of men have been changed." See *Journal of the Sixteenth General Assembly* (1964), pp.141–42. White Nazarenes in the Republic of South Africa grappled with similar issues, which British missionaries David Hynd and Kenneth Bedwell addressed in the booklet *Holiness and Race Relations and Holiness Evangelism Among the Europeans* (1942).

[19] See H. Richard Niebuhr's *Christ and Culture* (New York: Harper and Row, 1951).

missionaries of an earlier era, Americans in cross-cultural settings are sometimes viewed as cultural imperialists, and their ability to succeed depends on their willingness to become servants of others. This aspect of modern American culture raises an important question: what is the role of American leadership in a diverse international church in which Americans are now less than one-third? Will Americans share leadership roles with others? Can they accept the leadership of Nazarenes from non-Western cultures whose life experiences are often so very different?

The Western world's culture of affluence represents a different challenge posed by the idols of materialism, technology, and the modern media. Using sensuous messages, corporations tell us that we are primarily sexual beings who can find happiness through buying their products. The popular entertainments of an affluent culture can devolve into mere escapism or worse. The culture of affluence insulates middle-class people in the Western world from the poor, affecting their attitude toward the poor in their own countries and toward the poor in other nations. Does personal contact with the poor increase our Christian compassion or erode it? Are we more likely, or less likely, to affirm with Bresee that the Church of the Nazarene exists for "the salvation of souls and relief of the needy"? The modern news media makes us vividly aware of the world's great human needs, yet we often remain stingy. Has affluence posed the truest test of our Christian character? Is the real crisis over holiness theological in nature, or is it, instead, the temptation to selfishness and a failure of costly discipleship?

American culture has affected the trajectory of Nazarene history for both good and ill. Western Nazarenes generally, and American Nazarenes in particular, are called to sift their culture from the standpoint of Christocentric priorities.

INTERNATIONALIZATION

In the last quarter-century, *internationalization* emerged as a significant factor in the church's trajectory, and as a counter-weight to the influence of American culture. The church's early mission efforts led to strong work in India, China, Japan, Swaziland, South Africa, Central and South America, and the Caribbean, and a small but important presence in the Middle East. Financial downturns led to retrenchment in the 1930s that involved closing mission stations, such as that in Eastern India (now Bangladesh). Nevertheless, the church managed to build and equip hospitals in China, India and Swaziland during this period, demonstrating a continuing belief that the salvation of souls should be accompanied by the relief of the needy. The financial picture brightened considerably after World War II as the American economy, in high gear, helped expand the church treasury. New missions in the 1950s led to new fields in the Philippines, South Korea, and other places. The Nazarenes attracted indigenous churches in Australia and Italy, and by 2010, its posture toward world evangelization led to organized work in nearly 145 nations.

The 1980 General Assembly's decision to embrace *internationalization* was an important development within that context. That decision—to hold Nazarenes together in one international church rather than break into national or regional churches—was an unprecedented development for a religious body with American origins. In 2010, only 33 percent of Nazarenes were Americans, and over 80 percent of the church's districts were outside the U.S. and Canada. At the 2001 General Assembly, 43 percent of the delegates present and voting spoke English as their second language or did not speak it at all. Internationalization has created a church that may have the most diverse general meeting of any Protestant denomination in the world. No one knows how this experiment will end. But as it stands presently, internationalization embodies the conviction that Christ has opened the church to those of all nations, ages, and races.

LESSONS OF NAZARENE HISTORY
The trajectory of Nazarene history is full of lessons. We will identify three. First, the future always grows out of the past, even when it does so in ways that are not anticipated. The missionaries and mission executives who launched the Church of the Nazarene on a mission to the world never clearly discerned the ways in which internationalization would be an outcome. Their hopes were bounded by the ideas of their time and culture, and yet internationalization was a direct outgrowth and consequence of the work they initiated.

Second, no matter how much the founders are valued in the abstract, their vision may not endure. The ideal of an apostolic ministry that included those of both genders was a non-negotiable for them. This shared notion of the three major parent-bodies separated them from other churches but drew them together into union. The decline of women in ministry in the church's second half-century represented more than simply a bias against women. It represented a rejection of the theology of ministry and the emphasis on apostolicity that the founders had embraced.

Third, Nazarenes have a distinctive story, but that story is also part of a wider one—a truly Christian story with an evangelical subtext. The Nazarene story is rooted in Methodist antecedents and in the broader history of American and global evangelicalism. In that ocean in which we swim, we do not swim alone.

Chapter 2
Christian Baptism and the Early Nazarenes:
The Sources that Shaped a Pluralistic Baptismal Tradition

"Unity in essentials; liberty in nonessentials." Around the principle embedded in this old aphorism, the founders of the Pentecostal Church of the Nazarene merged three separate denominations into one.

The three churches originated in different sections of the American nation: the Association of Pentecostal Churches of America along the eastern seaboard, the Holiness Church of Christ in the South and Southwest (merger of New Testament Church of Christ and the Independent Holiness Church), and the Church of the Nazarene on the Pacific coast. Despite their diverse and independent points of origin, the three groups were already united on significant issues before their merger. Each held firmly to the Wesleyan way of salvation and Christian life as modified by the American holiness movement. Each embraced pietism as its dominant spiritual mode and accepted the modifications that American revivalism made to the pietist tradition. All three churches ordained women, had female pastors, and affirmed a common theological basis for doing so.

Likewise, each was a *believers' church,* exhibiting the traits of a distinctive style of churchmanship whose classic characteristics were enumerated by Donald F. Durnbaugh in *The Believers' Church: The History and Character of Radical Protestantism* (1968). Durnbaugh argued that the believers' church is a voluntary fellowship based on the idea of separation from the world and the gathering together of converted believers, rejecting the notion of the visible church as a mixed assembly of the regenerate and unregenerate. The believers' church emphasizes the necessity for all members to be active in Christian work. It practices church discipline. Its members care for the poor, especially those Christian sisters and brothers in need. It follows a simple pattern of worship and centers its common life on "the Word, prayer, and love."¹

With varying degrees of emphasis, the uniting groups of 1907–1908 reflected the characteristics of the believers' church tradition, and each did so with specific reference over-and-against episcopal Methodism, the nation's largest Protestant tradition. The "northern" branch, the Methodist Episcopal Church, was America's largest Protestant church. The Methodist Episcopal Church, South, was the second largest. Together, the twin denominations were developing into the quintessential American denomination.

There remained differences between and within the regional holiness denominations, and these were reconciled by the principle of "liberty in nonessentials." The 1898 *Manual* of Phineas Bresee's Church of the Nazarene in the West makes clear that "essentials" were beliefs "necessary" to salvation.² Particular eschatologies and baptismal views were nonessentials, requiring liberty of conscience. Were these doctrines then deemed unimportant? Hardly so. If educator A. M. Hills held staunchly to post-millennialism, Southern churchman J. B. Chapman and others were pre-millenialists with equal conviction. Did general superintendents Bresee and H. F. Reynolds affirm the importance of infant baptism? Rescue worker J. T. Upchurch disdained that doctrine and practice.³ In the newly organized Pentecostal Church of the Nazarene, liberty of conscience was required precisely because particular baptismal and eschatological views were affirmed strongly—so strongly, in fact, that it was pointless for any one school of thought on these issues to seek prevalence in church councils over those holding contrary views. The practice of pluralism was not indifference to doctrines like baptism and eschatology, but its opposite. It was rooted in the steadfast conviction that Pentecostal Nazarene unity should necessarily establish its focus elsewhere—on the Wesleyan way of salvation, in particular.

---

¹ Donald F. Durnbaugh, *The Believers' Church: The History and Character of Radical Protestantism* (New York: The Macmillan Company, 1970), pp. 4, 32–33.
² See *Manual of the Church of the Nazarene; Promulgated by the Assembly of 1898 held in Los Angeles, Cal.* (Los Angeles: Committee of Publication [of the Church of the Nazarene], n.d.), p.10.
³ The post-millennialism of A. M. Hills is presented, among other places, in his *Fundamental Christian Theology. A Systematic Theology*, 2 vols. (Pasadena, Cal.: C. J. Kinne, 1931), II: 339, 351–60. Chapman's pre-millenial views are stated in the same volume, pp. 339–51. The practice of infant baptism by Bresee and Reynolds is documented toward the end of this essay. J. T. Upchurch's antagonism to infant baptism is verified in *The Holiness Evangel* (June 1, 1907): 1.

Two questions bear examination within this context: what were the actual baptismal traditions of the uniting churches, and what did the embrace of pluralism in baptismal theology bring to the Pentecostal Nazarene synthesis?

BAPTISMAL THEOLOGY IN THE HOLINESS CHURCH OF CHRIST

The Holiness Church of Christ was the Southern root of the Pentecostal Church of the Nazarene, and it brought to the church union the largest number of congregations. Itself the product of an earlier merger, the Holiness Church of Christ had two parent bodies, and a different baptismal tradition emerged in each. One baptismal tradition was broad and inclusive, while the other was focused and exclusive. These opposing attitudes were reconciled in 1904 at Rising Star, Texas, when the two Southern holiness churches united, each committing itself in the process to the principle of pluralism of baptismal expression, while insisting that Christian baptism was a necessary pre-condition for church membership.

Robert Lee Harris (left) and Phineas Bresee represented two different ways of thinking about Christian baptism. Harris insisted that pouring was the only Scriptural mode, but Bresee considered sprinkling, pouring, and immersion to all be Scriptural and acted accordingly, letting the candidate for baptism decide the mode.

A narrow and restrictive theology of baptism was held by the New Testament Church of Christ, a restorationist body that originated in western Tennessee. The New Testament Church of Christ was a form of Free Methodism indigenized and fitted to the Southern context. Robert Lee Harris, its founder, encountered Free Methodism in Texas in the early 1880s, was sanctified under its auspices, entered the Holiness Movement through its doors, joined its clergy, and was ordained deacon and elder by B. T. Roberts, its founding general superintendent. Harris was a valued evangelist in the Texas Conference of the Free Methodist Church, but his enthusiasm for independent self-supporting foreign missions put him at odds with denominational agencies. He withdrew in 1889, uniting with a Southern Methodist congregation in Memphis. Harris continued his evangelistic career, using a local preacher's license as the new basis of his ministerial authority. He was then involved in "the evangelist controversy" in Southern Methodism, where he was again drawn into conflict with denominational authority. Another source also fueled Harris' tension with Southern Methodism: as he itinerated, he propagated Free Methodism's distinctive spirituality that was united to restrictive personal ethics and, in many instances, liberal social doctrines. Harris searched for an answer to his ecclesiastical dilemma throughout his five years in the Southern Methodist church. He now lived in an area that was highly conducive to restorationist views. Memphis was the home of Baptist controversialist James Graves and a center for the dissemination of Landmark Baptist doctrines. The people of western Tennessee were also conversant with the restorationist views of the Christian Church, known popularly as Campbellites, Disciples of Christ, and the Church of Christ. But Harris' new movement differed sharply from Baptists and Campbellites by uniting the spiritual and moral vision of Free Methodism to a restorationist base.[4]

Baptismal theology was an important element in the new holiness sect that sprang from Harris' ministry. The New Testament Church of Christ took shape during May and June of 1894 as Harris preached a series of sermons in Milan, Tennessee, on "the church question," or the relationship of Wesleyan holiness people to the "popular churches." According to the unpublished diary of Donie Mitchum, Harris "unmasked sin in and out of the churches and showed all sects and denominations to be unscriptural." Afterwards, he preached a series on "justification, sanctification, second coming of Christ, and how our souls were fed. After [that,] he preached a sermon on pouring as the scriptural mode of Baptism." This last sermon provoked a public challenge from a local Campbellite, so Harris dedicated a series of services to debating baptismal theology with his challenger. From this debate, Harris gained a new and significant convert, a Baptist deacon named Robert Balie Mitchum.[5] One month later, on July 5, 1894, the New Testament Church of Christ was "set in order," a phrase meaning

---

[4] Robert Lee Harris' Free Methodist background and its impact on his Southern Methodist ministry and on the creation of the New Testament Church of Christ are detailed in chapters 4 and 5 of Robert Stanley Ingersol, "Burden of Dissent: Mary Lee Cagle and the Southern Holiness Movement," unpublished Ph.D. dissertation, Duke University, 1989.

[5] The Journal of Donie Adams Mitchum, unpublished manuscript, p.17. MF copy in the Donie and Robert Balie Mitchum Collection, Nazarene Archives, Lenexa, Kansas. Balie Mitchum became a significant lay leader in the New Testament Church of Christ and the Holiness Church of Christ. He was the president of the latter at the union General Assembly of 1908 at Pilot Point, Texas. In 1923, he was a founding member of the church's

that the church of which Christ alone is founder already existed among the Christian people and was being recognized and structured along scriptural lines. In a service held four days later, Harris summarized the government and doctrines of the New Testament church, called for new members to step forward, and re-baptized those whose previous baptism was by immersion. The identities of two of these are known. One was Donie Mitchum, a lifelong Methodist who taught the young girls' Sunday school class at the Methodist church. Balie Mitchum, her Baptist husband, was another.[6] A Memphis newspaper reported the new church's doctrines, and Harris' view of baptism was stated succinctly: "The baptism of the Holy Ghost was administered by pouring, and therefore as water baptism is a likeness of the baptism of the Holy Ghost, it also must be administered by pouring."[7]

The earliest available exposition of this baptismal theology was published in the 1900 *Guidebook* of the Texas Council of the New Testament Church of Christ. Article 10, on baptism, is identical to the wording that appeared in the Memphis newspaper, and therefore bears Robert Lee Harris' direct stamp. The article is followed by a series of scripture texts, each dealing primarily with the outpouring of the Holy Spirit (Acts 2:15–18; Acts 10:44–48; Acts 11:15–16; and Joel 2:28).[8] More than three pages of discussion followed. This is significant, for baptism was the only doctrinal point given exposition in the entire manual! The case for pouring as the scriptural mode was stated in three points: (1) "The baptism of the Holy Spirit was promised to believers throughout this dispensation." (2) Spirit baptism is *real* baptism, while water baptism "is called baptism" because its design is to be "the likeness, or picture, of real baptism." Harris argued: "Wine was called the blood of Christ when drank [sic] to represent it, yet it was not the blood in reality, but it wore the name of the thing it [depicted] … so it is with water baptism. If it is not … [done in a mode that depicts] the real baptism, it is no more baptism than wine, when drank [sic] without reference to the blood of Christ, is

---

General Board. After leaving Milan, he became the founder and president of two successful companies in Nashville.

[6] Donie Mitchum's Journal, pp. 19–20; "The Church of Christ," *Milan (Tenn.) Exchange* (July 7, 1894): 4; and "Organized His Church," ibid. (July 14, 1894): 4. The Mitchums' daughter Hazel did not require rebaptism; she had been baptized by pouring at age six in the parlor of the Mitchum home in a service performed by Mrs. Mitchum's brother, T. L. Adams, a Southern Methodist minister and holiness evangelist. For that account, see Donie Mitchum's Journal, unnumerated pages inserted inside the front cover.

[7] Donie Mitchum's Journal, clipping, p. 23.

[8] *Government and Doctrines of New Testament Churches* (Waco, Texas: The Evangelist Publishing Company, 1900), pp. 24–25.

blood." (3) Real baptism consists of the Spirit, the baptismal event, and the mode of outpouring. In water baptism, water symbolizes the Spirit, and the mirror image of Spirit baptism is by pouring. Article 11 defined *who* could baptize—vesting that authority in a duly recognized minister, but adding that "under circumstances of necessity a simple disciple may administer baptism."[9] There was no printed baptismal ritual, nor any indication of whether infants could be baptized.

Robert Lee Harris died five months after the New Testament Church of Christ was formed. The trajectory of his movement was subsequently altered by that fact. Harris created a church in which ecclesiology and soteriology were jointly determinative doctrines in a theological system, but the gravity of theological weight shifted in the hands of his successors, who increasingly subordinated ecclesiological values to soteriological ones. Theological transformation occurred within the sect over the course of the next decade.[10]

As the New Testament Church of Christ expanded, its baptismal doctrine inhibited its growth within a Southern religious culture steeped in immersionist thinking. This was recognized early in the sect's history and led to a reconsideration of the church's baptismal doctrines when the first connectional council met in 1899. The discussion grew quite heated. The founder's widow, Mary Lee Harris (soon to become Mary Lee Cagle), insisted that her late husband's founding principles should be maintained without amendment. Others strongly disagreed. Donie Mitchum wrote in her private journal that Mary Harris "would not yield an inch but rather manifested (apparently) an ugly spirit. All other talks were made in the spirit of Christ. My sympathy goes out for her as she has much to overcome on the line of having her way about things." After debating the issue three separate times, the council reaffirmed pouring as the scriptural view but recognized that:

> there are saved people in [God's] church who give evidence of the same by their godly walk and conversation who have been immersed, and we recognize them as God's children and we as a part of His household cannot afford to turn away those He accepts ... [A]s we are

---

[9] Ibid., pp. 25–29.
[10] In Ingersol, "Burden of Dissent," there is discussion of the relationship between the New Testament Church of Christ and the Church of God (Holiness), another holiness-restorationist body, including ordination of elders in the New Testament Church of Christ by Church of God ministers. There is also discussion of *why* these two groups, with similar ecclesiologies, followed different trajectories of development. See pp. 165–68.

congregational in government it is left with each local congregation to say whether or not they accept or reject members who believe in and practice immersion and have not been baptized by pouring.[11]

On this basis, the sect's churches in Tennessee and Arkansas continued to baptize by pouring but opened the way for individuals previously baptized by other modes to unite with New Testament Church congregations that were willing to receive them without rebaptism.

This adjustment applied only to the Eastern Council of the New Testament Church of Christ. Before this time, Mary Lee Cagle had organized congregations in Texas, and in 1902 she formed these into a separate Texas Council. There, baptism by pouring remained a condition of membership, though it became a contested issue in 1903. That year, the Texas Council debated a motion that read: "Resolved, that we do not make the mode of water baptism a test of church membership." The resolution was defeated, but the issue was reopened the following day after the council learned that some congregations had accepted, without rebaptism, members previously baptized by other modes. The council president ruled that such persons were not members, and this ruling stood. Rev. J. W. Manney, who led attempts to change the rule, then reported "that he had set in order a congregation at Chilton, Texas, composed of 30 members, all of whom agreed to submit to the ruling of the Council on the baptism question."[12] Thus, the Eastern and Texas Councils of the New Testament Church of Christ remained in agreement on pouring as the scriptural mode of baptism, but differed on whether rebaptism was required to receive into membership those already baptized by other modes.

During this period, the New Testament Church of Christ moved toward merger with the Independent Holiness Church led by Charles B. Jernigan and James B. Chapman. Jernigan, a consummate organizer, believed in casting wide nets. In 1901, he helped organize both the Holiness Association of Texas, an interdenominational body, and the Independent Holiness Church, a sectarian one. In justifying the rise of the Independent Holiness Church, Jernigan stated repeatedly that its people sought "a place where the sacraments could be administered." In his view, the scattered holiness bands in East Texas needed to be organized into churches because

---

[11] Official Journal of the Church of Christ, unpublished ms., New Testament Church of Christ Collection, Nazarene Archives, pp. 3–4; Donie Mitchum's Journal, p.115.

[12] See *Texas Annual Council, New Testament Church of Christ: Second Session; held at Roby, Texas, Nov. 26–29, 1903* (n.p., n.d.), unpaginated. See "Second Day–Afternoon Session," Resolution No. 2, and the discussion following. Also see "Third Day–Evening Session."

in the bands "there was no baptism, no sacraments for her people, and they were called come-outers by the church people." The Independent Holiness Church recognized all modes of baptism as valid and scriptural, though Chapman, at least, preferred immersion. According to critic B. F. Neely, they also accepted unbaptized Christians into membership.[13]

In the late summer of 1904, Jernigan sought the merger of three Southern churches: the Independent Holiness Church, the New Testament Church of Christ, and the Holiness Baptist Churches of Arkansas organized and led by W. J. Walthall of Texarkana. In sharp contrast to the New Testament Church of Christ, the Holiness Baptists were strict immersionists. Jernigan's liberal position was obviously the only valid basis for a merger of the three bodies. At their annual council in late September, the Holiness Baptists expressed very strong interest in consolidating with other holiness churches, but only if immersion were the *exclusive* mode of baptism.[14] The other two denominations went forward without the Holiness Baptists, gathering at a delegated meeting in November at Rising Star, Texas. There, Mary Lee Cagle and her protégé, B. F. Neely, defended pouring as the scriptural mode, but agreed ultimately to a compromise in which both groups made concessions. The two churches agreed that in the new Holiness Church of Christ, baptism would be required for church membership, but mode would be left to the individual conscience. Jernigan's published account of the Rising Star council declared baptism a "nonessential." What did he mean, exactly? In context, it meant that different modes of baptism could be accommodated in the search for unity in holiness, though baptism itself was a requirement, in their view, for a person's identification with the visible church. This point was even strengthened in the *Manual* of 1906, when a sentence was added following

---

[13] Charles B. Jernigan, *Pioneer Days of the Holiness Movement in the Southwest* (Kansas City: Pentecostal Nazarene Publishing House, 1919), pp. 109 and 123; on Chapman's preference for immersion, see *Herald of Holiness* (Jan.10, 1923): 3, and (Feb. 7, 1923): 3. As settlers in Oklahoma Territory in early 1899, Chapman's family drew close to the Disciples of Christ Church. Chapman writes that later that year "one of my sisters and my mother joined the Christian Church and were baptized, putting in their membership at Soldier Creek." Chapman's account is reprinted in D. Shelby Corlett, *Spirit Filled: The Life of The Rev. James Blaine Chapman, D.D.* (Kansas City: Beacon Hill Press, n.d.), p. 25. Perhaps Chapman was influenced directly by Disciples of Christ baptismal theology in which "immersion" was considered synonymous with "baptism" and John the Baptist was often called "John, the Immerser."

[14] "Annual Convocation of Holiness Baptist Churches," *Pentecostal Herald* (Oct. 26, 1904): 6, and Jernigan, *Pioneer Days*, pp. 122–23. While the Holiness Baptists did not enter the merger, there were ministers and lay people who united individually, including Rev. Dora Rice, later a companion and mentor to Agnes White Diffee, and Rev. E. R. Morgan, later a Nazarene district superintendent.

that on freedom of mode. The new line declared: "This article can in no wise be construed to mean, that one can be admitted into the congregation without water baptism."[15]

BAPTISM AND THE ASSOCIATION OF PENTECOSTAL CHURCHES OF AMERICA

Like the Holiness Church of Christ, the Association of Pentecostal Churches of America stood in the believers' church tradition. Like its Southern sister, it was also the product of a merger. No single manual bound this denomination together, for each congregation wrote its own. Like many Baptist denominations, this one was a union of congregations united by common theology, mutual support between churches, educational and publishing interests, and a strong sense of mission to the world. Except for a lengthy statement on entire sanctification, the doctrinal statement of the denomination is quite brief. The one short reference to baptism states that it is the "initiatory rite" of the visible church. Our method here, then, must be to analyze baptismal statements found in the various congregational manuals.

The earliest branch in the East was the Central Evangelical Holiness Association, a small New England denomination formed in 1890 by ten independent congregations all less than four years old. One of these was the People's Evangelical Church of Providence, Rhode Island, that formed in 1887 under the leadership of Fred Hillery. Hillery founded a vital church paper, *The Beulah Christian,* which functioned after 1890 as a connectional organ for the New England churches, and after 1897 as the official organ of the Association of Pentecostal Churches of America. The 1895 manual of the People's Evangelical Church resonates with the key themes of the believers' church tradition. The opening paragraph states:

> A church consists of a number of believers who unite themselves by a public profession of the Christian religion, and by mutual covenant, to pray together and watch over one another in love, to maintain the worship

---

[15] "Union of Holiness Churches," *Pentecostal Herald* (Dec. 7, 1904): 4; and Jernigan, *Pioneer Days*, p. 123. Also see the *Manual of the Holiness Church of Christ, 1904–1905,* esp. pp. 15–16. On Neely's role, see notes of Timothy L. Smith's conversation with him, August 10, 1955, in the Timothy L. Smith Collection, Nazarene Archives. Neely was baptized by Mary Lee Cagle in 1901. At Rising Star, he took the position that he "could not and would not join a church that rejected water baptism—one of Christ's commands." Also see Smith, *Called Unto Holiness* (Kansas City: Nazarene Publishing House, 1962), pp. 170–71, where he draws out the significance of the water baptism issue in the merger process at Rising Star. On the addition to the article on baptism, see the 1906 *Manual,* p. 19.

and service of God, and the ordinances and discipline of the gospel.[16]

The manual contains a Confession of Faith. Three of its eleven articles concern the church and the sacraments (Articles VII, VIII, and IX). Two of these are quoted in their entirety:

> **ARTICLE VII:** We believe that Christ has a visible church in the world, that its ordinances are Baptism and the Lord's Supper; that the Christian Sabbath and the Gospel Ministry are institutions of divine appointment, and that it is the duty of Christians to unite with this visible church and observe its sacred ordinances.
>
> **ARTICLE VIII:** We believe that the outward sign in Baptism is water applied in the name of the Father, and the Son, and the Holy Ghost; that the inward grace signified in this ordinance is a death unto sin and a new birth unto righteousness.[17]

A good deal is left unsaid. Were infants baptized, and was mode of baptism an issue? Was baptism a condition of church membership? Taking the last question first, Christian baptism was indeed required. Article VII stated clearly that the visible church's ordinances are two in number, and that "it is the duty of Christians to unite with this visible church and observe its sacred ordinances." The congregational covenant gave this general principle concrete application, a line of it stating: "We do covenant to attend the worship of God and the ordinances of the gospel with this Church." Moreover, a baptism ritual is integrated into the ritual for church membership. The point in the membership ritual where baptism occurs is placed in brackets, indicating the option of omission, but the option would be for new members who had been baptized previously. Indeed, the means of grace were valued so highly that Standing Rules 10 and 11 made their neglect, including "unnecessary absence" from communion, a ground for church discipline and dismissal. Two other items are worth noting. First, the manual required the church clerk to keep a "chronological register of all members showing name and date of those baptized." Second, the church

---

[16] *Manual of the People's Evangelical Church of Providence, R.I.* (Providence: Office of the Beulah Christian, 1895), p. 3.
[17] Ibid., p. 8.

had five committees, and one of these was the Baptism Committee. The Manual set forth its duties:

> The committee shall arrange things necessary for the proper observance of this ordinance, and, if the mode of baptism selected by the candidate be immersion, furnish suitable dresses and proper conveyance to and from the water.

Mode of baptism was clearly a matter of individual conscience. The manual also reflects many other marks of the believers' church tradition. There was a Sick and Destitute Committee composed of nine members. Its duties included visiting the sick, the infirm and the destitute; furnishing watchers for the sick; providing for the needy from the funds at their disposal; and assisting the unemployed to find suitable employment.[18] This and other such characteristics reinforce the idea that Christian baptism was understood as initiation into a community of devotion, service, and love.

The year after the People's Evangelical Church organized, a sister congregation formed in Lynn, Massachusetts. A manual dated 1898 contains a Confession of Faith identical to that of the People's Church, including three identical articles on the church and sacraments.[19] Everything else in the Lynn church's manual is different, including its church covenant and standing rules, though evidence of the believers' church tradition again abounds. The church Constitution established regular covenant meetings as a specific type of meeting distinct from business and prayer meetings. The significance of the covenant meeting was underscored by its relationship to the sacrament of communion: "The covenant meeting should be held the last Friday evening before the first Sunday in every month, and the Holy Communion should be celebrated on the succeeding Lord's Day."[20] The Lynn congregation vested oversight of baptism in the Official Board of the church, assigning it the task of

---

[18] See the church's Covenant, ibid., pp. 4–5; for the baptismal covenant and vows, see pp. 27–28; on Standing Rules related to neglect of the means of grace, see pp. 12–13; on the registry of baptisms, see p. 18; on the Baptism Committee and other committees, see pp. 19–22. An interesting feature of the internal organization of the People's Church was the division of the entire membership into Methodist type classes that met weekly under the direction of class leaders. Among other duties, the class leaders were to "consult with the pastor for the welfare of the Church," take charge of worship in the pastor's absence, and prepare and assist in administering the Lord's Supper. See ibid., pp. 10, 17–18.
[19] *Manual of the First Pentecostal Church of Lynn, Mass.* (Providence, R.I.: Pentecostal Printing Co., 1898), pp. 8–12.
[20] Ibid., p. 14.

examining candidates and making necessary preparations for observing the rite. Nothing more of baptism appears in this manual, but the believers' church tradition is the context for the observance of both sacraments. For instance, the Lynn church's emphasis on mutual support is reflected in the fact that among its five committees were a Committee on Sick and Poor and a Committee on Hospitality.[21]

In 1897, the Central Evangelical Holiness Association, including these member churches at Providence and Lynn, united with the Association of Pentecostal Churches of America, an organization formed in 1895 under the leadership of William Howard Hoople of Brooklyn, New York. Both merging groups were congregational in government. Each ordained ministers subject to a congregational vote and the examination and laying on of hands by a presbytery of ministers.[22] Hoople's wing of the merger was vital and growing but may have lacked theological depth, since some of the later congregational manuals of the united body contain confessions of faith modeled after the confessions of the older New England churches. The name of Hoople's group was more geographically inclusive, so it became the name under which the two bodies united. Though it originated on the Eastern seaboard, it did not remain confined there. By 1907 the denomination had congregations extending from Nova Scotia down through New England and the Mid-Atlantic states, and then westward north of the Ohio River as far as Iowa.

The congregational manuals for churches in New York and Pennsylvania that stemmed from Hoople's sphere of influence tend to say less about baptism. One example is the manual of the Lincoln Place Pentecostal Church in Pennsylvania that was organized in 1899. Its 1904 manual contains a single article (Article VIII) on the church and its sacraments, referring to the latter simply as "the initiatory and memorial rites, Baptism, and the Lord's Supper." A lengthy exposition of the article follows but deals solely with establishing a theological basis for the independence of the local church. This manual carries no rituals, and its only other mention

---

[21] Ibid., pp. 15–17.

[22] The ordination practices of the Central Evangelical Holiness Association are clear from ordination accounts published in the *Beulah Christian*, 1890–1894, passim. These show that congregations selected a candidate for minister, and that a panel of ministers from sister churches examined and ordained the candidate. In the united church after 1897, explicit guidelines outline the ordination process, including the statement that ordination will be "by the laying on of the hands of the presbytery." See Article VII under "Summary of Doctrines" in *Association of Pentecostal Churches of America, Minutes of the Sixth Annual Meeting* (Providence, R.I.: Pentecostal Printing Company, 1901), p. 58. The ordination credential of John Norberry, in the Nazarene Archives, has the term "presbytery" in its text and bears the signatures of the ordaining ministers.

of baptism is to vest the church advisory board with the task of examining candidates for baptism.[23]

By 1900, however, a generic manual circulated among some churches in the Association of Pentecostal Churches of America. The generic manual was a template that new congregations could adopt or modify, and at least two congregations adopted it whole—one in Vermont, and another in Nova Scotia. The generic manual provides the most detailed glimpse available into baptismal practices among the churches of the Northeast. It includes separate rituals for infant baptism and believer's baptism. The ritual for infants appealed to Jesus' welcoming the little children. It then specified conditions for parents or sponsors, including teaching the child to know the "nature and end of this holy sacrament." Children were to be taught to give "reverent attendance upon the means of grace," specifically public and private worship, the ministry of preaching, and Bible study. The ritual for believer's baptism was strikingly different. It began with a narrative of Nicodemus' conversation with Jesus on the distinction between water and Spirit, moved to the renunciation of the devil and his works, affirmed the Apostles' Creed, and ended in a vow of obedience to the commandments of God. The generic manual specifically recognized sprinkling, pouring, and immersion as valid modes, leaving the choice of mode to the candidate.[24]

The Beulah Christian reported a variety of baptismal practices in use throughout the denomination. In 1893, Rev. H. N. Brown conducted a service in Keene, New Hampshire, in which he "baptized five children, received two adults on probation, and administered the Lord's Supper." In a different vein, the church at Malden, Massachusetts, conducted a baptism service in 1895 in which three adults were immersed. One reads that "the service was impressive."[25]

---

[23] *Articles of Faith and Government of the Lincoln Place Pentecostal Church* of Lincoln Place, Pa. (Providence: Pentecostal Publishing Company, 1904), pp. 10–11, 18. This congregation's manual required a monthly communion observance; see ibid., p. 17.
[24] The generic manual was adopted by two congregations for certain: First Pentecostal Church of Johnson, Vt., and Second Pentecostal Church of Oxford, Nova Scotia. Copies of each are in the Nazarene Archives. The Oxford congregation personalized its manual with a special cover bearing the church name. On the rituals for infants and adults, see either manual, pp. 14–17; on mode of baptism, see esp. p. 17. Other manuals with the identical ritual include that of the Pentecostal Mission Church, West Somerville, Mass. (1901), the First Pentecostal Church of Lowell, Mass. (1904), and the *Discipline of Ebenezer Pentecostal Church of Allentown, Penn.* (n.d.). (The latter was a congregation formed by former members of the Evangelical Association.) An expanded form of the same ritual appears in the manual of the First People's Church of Brooklyn, N.Y. (1907).
[25] *Beulah Christian* (Sept. 1893): 2 and (Oct. 1895): 2.

Baptismal practices within the Association of Pentecostal Churches of America can be summarized as follows. First, each congregation was at liberty to shape its own theological statement about the meaning and significance of baptism. Second, the denominational framework allowed the widest latitude, permitting infant and believer's baptism, and leaving the choice of mode to the candidate's conscience. Third, the fact of pluralism meant that church members were expected to maintain a spirit of harmony with those who thought and acted differently on the subject. Fourth, all this was placed within the framework of a strong believers' church tradition that stressed a congregational covenant, church discipline, good works, and mutual support.

BAPTISM IN THE CHURCH OF THE NAZARENE IN THE WEST

In 1895, Phineas F. Bresee and J. P. Widney were elected co-pastors and general superintendents of a new congregation in Los Angeles. It was named the Church of the Nazarene, and it was established to provide the urban poor with the benefits of a family-oriented congregation. Widney was on the cusp of entering the ministry after a distinguished career as a physician and medical educator. He was a theological minimalist. By contrast, Bresee had nearly forty years of pastoral ministry experience and embraced a substantial theology. Widney separated from the Nazarenes in 1898, in conjunction with the first delegated assembly that brought together representatives from three congregations and several missions. This assembly authorized the first church manual bearing the "Church of the Nazarene" name. By 1903, Bresee envisioned an expanding network of churches and embarked on a deliberate plan of sect expansion that depended, partly, on the itinerant nation-wide ministry of evangelist C. W. Ruth, the church's assistant general superintendent. By 1907 there were over 50 congregations along the Pacific coast and as far east as Illinois.[26]

Bresee's basic theology was shaped by the Methodist Episcopal Church, in which he labored for 37 years. His ministry began on the Iowa prairies in 1857. Five years later, the conference's "Pastoral Address," written by its leading clergy, enumerated the challenges of pastoral ministry on the

---

[26] Widney played a crucial role in forming the Los Angeles Church of the Nazarene, including suggesting the church name that was adopted. He was, however, a classic religious dissenter. During his Nazarene years, his theological minimalism was confined to his dissatisfaction with creeds and his fascination with the simple teachings and example of Jesus. Later, he moved to a very different type of theological minimalism, rejecting the Christian theology of original sin, the Incarnation, and the Trinity. During his last thirty-five years, he was the pastor of an independent church known as the Church of the All-Father, and he adhered to a type of Unitarian Transcendentalism.

frontier. Specifically it touched on baptism and urged Iowa's Methodist people to "dedicate your children to God in baptism" and ignore the "sneer of those members of other denominations, who may differ with us on the doctrine of infant baptism, [and] make you ashamed to baptize the little ones God has given you." Historian Gayle Felton has identified how this emphasis on infant baptism functioned in nineteenth century Methodism. First, it underscored Methodist belief that children were included in God's covenant of salvation, and it functioned pastorally as a comfort to bereaved parents in a society characterized by high infant mortality. But it also functioned as a key component in Methodism's century-long struggle against Calvinism's advocates.

Reformed churches baptized infants but did so believing that not all were elected by God to salvation. Methodists, on the other hand, baptized infants believing that this sacrament underscored divine grace's universality and refuted Calvinists' notions of limited atonement. Methodists generally agreed that the Wesleyan logic implied that any child could be baptized; they also generally agreed that only the children of practicing Christian parents or guardians should be baptized under normal circumstances. Throughout his Methodist ministry, Bresee organized the "Baptized Children" of his congregations into classes under adult supervisors. The Methodist Episcopal *Discipline* required him and other pastors to do so. The baptized children were to "learn the nature and design of this sacrament" and receive instruction in the dynamics of Christian experience. They were to learn the obligations of Christian life, service, and piety that their baptism entailed. This background informed Bresee's baptismal theology and practice throughout his Nazarene years.[27]

The ecclesiology embodied in Bresee's 1898 *Manual* included one stark contrast with the ecclesiology of Robert Lee Harris' New Testament Church of Christ. Whereas Harris asserted that the Bible insisted on a specific plan of church government, the introduction to Bresee's first *Manual* states that the founders of the Pacific coast movement, "believing that the Lord Jesus Christ had ordained no particular form of government for the Church," were guided by "common consent" in framing their

---

[27] Carl O. Bangs, *Phineas F. Bresee: His Life in Methodism, the Holiness Movement, and the Church of the Nazarene* (Kansas City: Beacon Hill Press of Kansas City, 1995), quoted on p. 76. Gayle Carleton Felton, *This Gift of Water: The Practice and Theology of Baptism among Methodists in America* (Nashville: Abingdon Press, 1992), pp. 93–110. Regarding baptized children and the Methodist *Discipline*, a representative example of the church's official position during Bresee's ministry is found in the section titled "The Relation of Baptized Children to the Church" in *The Doctrines and Discipline of the Methodist Episcopal Church*, 1876, pp. 38–40.

polity, provided that nothing agreed upon was "repugnant to the Word of God."[28] Yet, the basis for also counting Bresee's group as a believers' church is unmistakable. The notion of being "gathered" is prominent. The introduction states that those who formed the first congregation in Los Angeles were "called of God to this work, to come out and stand together." They were called especially to live holy lives together, to minister to the poor and neglected, and to give active Christian testimony to their faith. Firm and explicit guidelines were given for applying church discipline.[29]

In Bresee's first *Manual*, the section on baptism is specific and liberal, affirming infant and believer's baptism as proper choices, allowing any mode of baptism, and allowing rebaptism "on account of uncertainty, or lack of proper instruction, or scruples having arisen as to mode." The rituals for infant and adult baptism state that it "is an external seal of the New Covenant," while the internal seal is the baptism with the Holy Spirit. In the case of infants, the external seal of baptism replaces the external seal of circumcision in the Old Covenant. The story of Jesus and the little children in Luke 18 was called to remembrance before the charge to parents or sponsors was read. Among the charges is the obligation of parents to teach the child "the design of this sacrament," the scriptures, and other things necessary to salvation.[30]

The ritual for baptizing adults made a more explicit connection between water and Spirit baptisms. The candidate was reminded that the baptism with the Holy Spirit is promised to all believers and will be fulfilled "in answer to obedient faith." Later in the ritual the candidate was asked: "Have you received the Holy Ghost since you believed—if not, do you now present yourself a living sacrifice to be cleansed from all sin?"[31] Thus a connection was made between water and Spirit baptism in which the former could function in some as a witness to prior Spirit baptism, and in others as anticipation of a future event.

The *Manual* of 1905–06 was the last manual of Bresee's church prior to its union with other holiness denominations. It shows unmistakable development and change in baptismal thinking and ritual within the span of seven years. In the later manual, the connection between water baptism and the Holy Spirit is no longer obvious, and the rite is now tied concretely to the declaration of saving faith. The ritual for believer's baptism has another change, too: the Apostles' Creed was now incorporated as part of

---

[28] *Manual* of the Church of the Nazarene, 1898, p. 10.
[29] Quotation from ibid., p. 9; also see pp. 10, 16–17, 20–21, 24, and 28–30.
[30] Ibid., pp. 22–23, 39–40.
[31] Ibid., pp. 40–41.

the baptismal covenant, identifying the act of baptism firmly with an early ecumenical creed, underlining the sacrament's catholicity.[32]

E. A. Girvin was Bresee's contemporary, confidant, and first biographer. In a general discussion of Bresee's use of ritual, Girvin turns to baptism and provides the reader with two insights into Bresee's typical practice. Girvin notes:

> His conduct of the baptismal service was especially helpful and edifying. He emphasized the duties and privileges of parents in rearing their children in the nurture and admonition of the Lord, and gave a beautiful exposition of the real spiritual significance of the ordinance of baptism. After performing the actual rite, he would take the little children in his arms and kiss them. This he did so lovingly that the hearts of the parents were always moved.[33]

Girvin portrays Bresee as the gentle pastor whose spirit and decorum elevated the occasion. But the passage is also reliable testimony that infant baptism was the norm at Los Angeles First Church throughout Bresee's tenure as its pastor. Bresee's pastoral practice remained consistent with the Methodist approach to baptism of his early ministry. Bresee's ability to edify the whole congregation through the practice of infant baptism underscores that it was, for him, truly *a sacrament of the church* in addition to being a means of grace for the individual.

Baptism was not an issue requiring negotiations between the Eastern, Western, and Southern churches, but it was raised as an issue at the 1907 General Assembly by Rev. Horace Trumbaur of the Pennsylvania Conference of the Holiness Christian Church. Trumbaur was a longtime associate of C. W. Ruth, who had left the Holiness Christian Church for the Church of the Nazarene in 1901. Trumbaur wanted to lead his people into the union of holiness churches, but he held strictly to believer's baptism. He was invited to sit with the assembly's Commission on Legislation. He told the story in his diary: "When I objected to infant baptism Dr. Bresee said to me: 'Would you object to other folks accepting it?'" Apparently Trumbaur and his people did not. The Pennsylvania Conference merged

---

[32] *Manual of the Church of the Nazarene ... 1905, with Changes Adopted at Assembly of 1906* (Los Angeles: Nazarene Publishing Company, n.d.), pp. 63–64.
[33] E. A. Girvin, *Phineas F. Bresee: A Prince in Israel* (Kansas City: Pentecostal Nazarene Publishing House, 1916), p. 386.

with the Pentecostal Church of the Nazarene in September 1908. Bresee did not feel compelled to make Trumbaur adjust his baptismal theology, but he was equally unwilling to allow Trumbaur's narrower view to extinguish his own theological vision.[34]

Bresee was flexible with respect to the settings in which baptism might occur. He baptized an infant at the beginning of the weekly Tuesday Holiness meeting. He baptized another child during a college convocation at Nazarene University. He baptized several children on Easter Sunday, 1904, and baptized a man at the church board's monthly meeting. He baptized at Sunday school picnics and conducted a specially-advertised baptism service at the beach "for a number of candidates." There was no baptistery in the "Glory Barn," a plain tabernacle-type structure where early Los Angeles Nazarenes first worshipped. This required C. W. Ruth, who was then Bresee's associate pastor, to use a nearby Methodist Episcopal Church to baptize a company of Los Angeles Nazarenes who had elected to be immersed.[35]

Bresee was flexible with respect to the timing, modes, and occasions for baptism, but the sacrament itself was always an important component in his approach to "shaping the Body of Christ."

Appropriating the Usable Past

An ongoing development of baptismal theology and practice characterized the regional groups that created the present-day Church of the Nazarene. Since the development of baptismal doctrine is a principle so well grounded in that early history, there should be no surprise that the new denomination's baptismal theology continued developing after 1908 and continues doing so today.

Second, this survey shows that a variety of baptismal expressions existed in each regional entity before any of them came together, and that each merging denomination arrived independently to a point where their baptismal practices and policies actually converged. Specifically, each merging denomination had reached a point by 1904 in which the validity of three different modes of baptism were affirmed and the choice of mode

---

[34] The H. G. Trumbaur Diary, entries for Oct. 9 and 14, 1907, in the Horace G. Trumbaur Collection, Nazarene Archives. For analysis, see Gordon Daniel Harris, "The Question of Infant Baptism in the Church of the Nazarene," unpublished M.A. thesis, Nazarene Theological Seminary, 2009, pp. 2, 43, 51–52. In contrast to Trumbaur's position, the Holiness Workers' Church, founded in 1898 in Canada by Frank Goff, affirmed infant baptism in its Articles of Religion. See: *The Doctrine and Discipline of the Holiness Workers' Church* (Clarksburg, Ontario: Office of the Holiness Worker, n.d. [circa 1910]), pp. 13–14.

[35] Bangs, *Phineas F. Bresee*, pp. 223, 232–34.

was left to the conscience of the candidate. The Eastern and Western denominations clearly permitted and routinely practiced infant baptism. Stories of infant baptism in the Holiness Church of Christ were not found, and yet the issues that needed to be negotiated between the Southern body and its two counterparts are well-known to scholars; infant baptism was not one of the points of contention. That fact can be coupled with the later well-documented practice of infant baptism on the Nazarene districts carved out of Holiness Church of Christ territory, providing strong evidence that infant baptism was also accepted within this denomination. The manner in which early Nazarenes embraced pluralism in baptismal theology and practice indicates that the focus of Nazarene unity rested on other points, namely those related to the Wesleyan way of salvation. Outside "the essentials," early Nazarenes not only tolerated but *expected* diversity of opinion and practice within their ranks.

Third, the founding churches were serious about the practice of baptism because they were serious about the church as a gathered and disciplined body of believers who testified to their faith through words and acts. Jernigan's insistence on the sacramental necessity for organizing the Independent Holiness Church was prompted by a concern to bring the signs and blessings of the visible church to the holiness bands, but it was also an implicit rebuke of the Methodist denominations that practiced (it was believed) the sacraments in increasingly undisciplined churches in which the means of grace were being steadily abandoned by the members. At first independently, and later as a unified body, the founding groups of the present-day Church of the Nazarene placed their baptismal theologies within the context of the believers' church tradition, with its emphasis on commitment and love.

The Church of the Nazarene did not adopt a formal Article of Faith on "The Church" until 1989. Nevertheless, definite ecclesiological assumptions lay behind the multiple separations of local bodies from Episcopal Methodism, and the coalescing of these groups into regional churches, then a national one, and, with the accession of the Pentecostal Church of Scotland in 1915, into an international one. The believers' church tradition lies at the very heart of early Nazarene experience, and thereby gives evidence that the Church of the Nazarene originated with a unique soul that brought together Methodist and believers' church emphases. Identifying this factor helps us better understand why the Nazarenes (and other Wesleyan holiness churches) came into existence, despite the fact that a majority of early twentieth-century Wesleyan holiness people remained loyal to the Methodist Episcopal churches. Moreover, this leading tension between the Methodist and believers' church poles has shaped the Church of the Nazarene's subsequent development.

As a believers' church in the Wesleyan tradition, early Nazarenes were not unlike American Episcopal Methodism in its first century and British Methodism from the death of John Wesley until the mid-twentieth century. Much like mainline Methodists, Nazarenes have risked destroying the character of their founders' vision, though by way of a much different trajectory. Whereas mainline Methodism now seems to reflect the full pluralism of American culture, the contemporary Church of the Nazarene has come to reflect the pluralism of American evangelicalism, much of it based on patterns of thought antithetical to Wesleyan ideas of scripture, salvation, and the means of grace. This tendency has influenced Nazarenes to accent ever more strongly the believers' church aspect of their tradition at the expense of the Wesleyan aspect. For this reason, attempts to "re-Wesleyanize" the church are regarded by some as necessary to restore the balance that was part of the founding vision.[36] A key part of the Nazarene theological task today may be to rediscover what it means to be a *believers' church* in the *Wesleyan* tradition. Indeed, this *may* be a theological need of the Wesleyan holiness denominations generally, though only a few thinkers (like Barry Callen and Howard Snyder) have shown any interest in doing so.[37] The neglect of this study tends to increase the distance between the church's theologians, who are interested primarily in the ways that Wesleyan principles connect with the broad Catholic tradition, and the emerging Nazarene churches in Asia, Africa, and Latin America, where the believers' church tradition is at the heart of new and growing Nazarene communities. Moreover, American Nazarene scholars tend to believe uncritically that a believers' church ethos necessarily entails a believer's baptism theology. Yet nothing is further from the truth. For centuries the Congregational and Presbyterian churches in Britain and America have demonstrated that infant baptism is fully compatible with a believers' church way of life. So, too, has the witness and practice of the many

---

[36] See, for instance, Paul Merritt Bassett's two related addresses: "Re-Wesleyanizing Nazarene Higher Education," Nazarene Faith, Learning, and Living Conference, 1985, San Diego, California, and "Toward An Agenda for Nazarene Theology," Seventh Nazarene Theology Conference, 1987, Kansas City, Missouri. Copies of these addresses are in the Paul Merritt Bassett Collection, Nazarene Archives, Lenexa, Kansas.

[37] Howard Snyder's series of books on ecclesiology draw freely, though not uncritically, from the believers' church tradition and other ecclesial traditions. Snyder is a Free Methodist. Barry Callen of the Church of God (Anderson, Ind.), and a longtime editor of the *Wesleyan Theological Journal*, identifies more self-consciously with the believers' church tradition. His most complete statement in this regard is the book *Radical Christianity: The Believers Church Tradition in Christianity's History and Future* (1999).

Methodist denominations around the world that have given a believers' church witness in a variety of different contexts: as "free churches" vis-à-vis the European state churches; as part of Christian religious minorities in Asia and Africa; and as part of Latin America's Protestant counter-culture. Moreover, without a conscious appraisal of the believers' church and its "high road" that Mennonite and Brethren scholars have long explored, a more individualistic "low road" within the believers' church tradition will be followed uncritically in Nazarene circles, as Baptist and Pentecostal strains of the tradition exert influence on aspects of Nazarene thought and life.

The point is nowhere better illustrated than in the long evolution of Nazarene baptismal practice, where the long-term trend was increasingly toward a predominant practice of believer's baptism, and increasingly by immersion. This has been true among American Nazarenes as the church has gravitated increasingly toward an Evangelical mainstream dominated in the twentieth century by Baptists and Pentecostals. But it is also true for large portions of the Church of the Nazarene in other world areas, particularly in Latin America, where believer's baptism is widely assumed by many evangelicals to be a counterweight to Roman Catholicism. In the church's 2009 General Assembly, a sizable contingent of delegates supported resolutions that sought to bring the Nazarenes into harmony with Baptist practices on both counts. While these efforts failed, they are likely to recur in subsequent general meetings. This trend is one of the strongest evidences that Nazarenes risk developing a Baptist soul and character at the expense of the founders' vision, losing that creative and meaningful tension that characterized early Nazarene faith and practice.

The restoration of that creative tension is available, however, through various means. One aspect of that process can be the joyful recovery and practice of pluralism in baptismal expression. As a matter of loyalty and respect for the consciences of lay people, each Nazarene pastor should be able and willing to articulate the theological basis behind each baptismal expression—infant baptism, believer's baptism, and the three modes—in a manner that lay people can understand.

The work of theologians is essential in re-examining the theological bases of these practices. Brief but useful summaries of Nazarene sacramental theology can be found in the works of H. Ray Dunning (*Grace, Faith & Holiness*, 1988) and J. Kenneth Grider (*A Wesleyan-Holiness Theology*, 1994). Still, the contribution of Rob L. Staples in *Outward Sign and Inward Grace* (1991) remains the most thorough and significant study of Nazarene sacramental theology written by any Nazarene scholar.

Theologically resourceful pastors also can assist the church. Jesse C. Middendorf's *The Church Rituals Handbook* (1997) provides a succinct but theologically satisfying statement on infant baptism. Brad Estep, a specialist in liturgical theology and practice, has also contributed through his study of "Baptismal Theology and Practice in the Church of the Nazarene: A Preservation of Plurality" (2000).[38]

The historian also has a role to play by calling to remembrance the people, words, and deeds that exemplify founding principles. For instance, the historian can call to remembrance the testimony of Mary King Snowbarger, the mother of Nazarene educators, who was baptized in Hutchinson, Kansas, nearly a century ago. In her oral history, she stated that Rev. H. M. Chambers "baptized Bertha, Esther, and myself at the same time as we knelt at the altar. He was using a pitcher and poured water on our heads. That has been a satisfactory baptism to me." S. S. White was another who was satisfied with his baptism. One of the founding faculty members of Nazarene Theological Seminary and the editor of the denominational paper, White later testified: "I was reared in the Methodist church and was baptized as a baby in my mother's arms. I have never doubted the validity of this baptism; I have been perfectly satisfied with it for many years."[39]

Another person to recall is Phineas Bresee, who was sought out at district assemblies to baptize infants, some of whom remained active church members to the very end of the twentieth century. Alpin Bowes was one such person. He was the infant child of San Diego First Church's pastor when Bresee baptized him and other babies at the 1915 Southern California District Assembly. Another, Alan Bresee Smith, was ordained at the Western Oklahoma District Assembly in 1914. Bresee was frail and sat in a chair, holding the infant between his knees while performing the rite.[40]

---

[38] Bradley Keith Estep, "Baptismal Theology and Practice in the Church of the Nazarene: A Preservation of Plurality," unpublished Ph.D. dissertation, Union Theological Seminary (Richmond, Virginia), 2000.

[39] Mary King Snowbarger, Autobiography, edited from interviews conducted by Willis Snowbarger, 1983, Transcript, Nazarene Archives, p. 11. And Stephen S. White, "Jesus' Baptism," *Herald of Holiness* (May 6, 1959): 12; quoted in Estep, "Baptismal Theology and Practice," p. 97.

[40] Alpin P. Bowes became an official in the denomination's Department of Home Missions in Kansas City, Missouri. Alan Bresee Smith became a Presbyterian minister and teacher and in 1989, lived in Osawatomie, Kansas. See: Alpin P. Bowes, memo to Stan Ingersol, Mar. 20, 1990, which quotes an extract from the unpublished diary of his father, Alpin G. Bowes; also see Alan B. Smith, letter to Stan Ingersol, Aug. 31, 1989.

Bresee was not the only founding general superintendent called upon for this honor. Hiram F. Reynolds was likewise pressed into willing service of this kind. Consider this notation in the 1924 *Journal* of the Eastern Oklahoma District: "At 2 o'clock Dr. Reynolds baptized six babies, which occasion was a blessing to all. After this a great ordination service followed." Or note these lines from the San Antonio District *Journal* of 1927: "Baptismal service followed. Dr. Reynolds called for all who wished to bring their children for baptism and seven were presented."[41] Similar statements can be found to demonstrate that infant baptisms were conducted in district assemblies by early general superintendents Roy T. Williams, J. B. Chapman, and John W. Goodwin, indicating the one-time popularity of the practice in a setting that held it, and its theological significance, up to a wide audience.[42]

District superintendents also baptized. In Southern California, W. C. Wilson baptized the baby of "Brother and Sister Stone," while N. B. Herrell of the Pittsburgh District conducted a service of Holy Communion followed by the baptism of three babies. Then, he noted, "the glory came streaming down." W. F. Rutherford, a superintendent in Texas, baptized "a nice class of babies" in Belton, Texas. After this, the local pastor preached a sermon that was followed by a second baptism service in which "baptism by immersion was administered" to adults. M. E. Borders baptized the baby of "Brother and Sister Russell Gray" after the love feast at the Sunday morning service of the Chicago District Assembly of 1916. Afterward, the assembly sang "A Charge to Keep I Have." Nearly thirty years later, Michigan District superintendent W. M. McGuire and missionary George J. Franklin immersed thirty people in the lake during a district assembly. "Shouts of victory were continuous throughout the service." Evangelists were also called upon to baptize people. In 1915, evangelists Theodore and Minnie Ludwig conducted revival services in Paola, Kansas, in which two infants and three adults were baptized. The following year, a pair of

---

[41] On H. F. Reynolds, see the *Journal of the Eastern Oklahoma District*, 1924: 16–17, and the *San Antonio District Journal*, 1927: 36. Also see the *Eastern Oklahoma District Journal*, 1928: 22.
[42] For references to infant baptisms conducted by general superintendent Roy T. Williams, see the *Journal* of the San Antonio District, 1921: 30, and ibid., 1926: 26; also the *Journal* of the Western Oklahoma District, 1931: 31, and ibid., 1934: 37; and the *Journal* of the Michigan District, 1945: 54. On an infant baptism conducted by J. B. Chapman, see the Western Oklahoma District Journal, 1929: 28. On John W. Goodwin, see ibid., 1932: 36; ibid., 1935: 45; and the San Antonio District Journal, 1936: 31.

female evangelists conducted "a beautiful baptismal service" in Durant, Oklahoma.[43]

Christian baptism was also an important part of life for early Nazarenes in other parts of the world. The noted Nazarene missionary, Harmon Schmelzenbach, reported in 1912 that he had "baptized three babies" one Sunday at the Grace Mission Station in Swaziland. In some cultures, missionaries preferred to hold mass baptisms. There were 118 people baptized in Kuang Ping Fu, China, on a Sunday in 1925. They were then received into church membership and partook of the Lord's Supper. On May 28, 1930, another 202 people were baptized at the Nazarene center in Tamingfu. Not all were local. Rev. C. J. Kinne noted that "they came from nearly all over our field." The last point was critical: mass baptisms shaped a sense of solidarity and reinforced the idea that Christian minorities possessed not only a common Christian faith but *also one another.* Baptisms in two other locations pushed the total number of Chinese baptized in May to 287. In 1936, Harry Wiese reported that 66 persons were baptized on a recent Sunday at Tamingfu. Some were sprinkled but the majority chose to be immersed in the church's baptistery. Missionaries spent the previous day interviewing the candidates, asking such questions as "their date of regeneration" and "if they are going to follow Jesus all the days of their life." These early mass baptisms would be replicated in other times and other countries. In 1984, there were 2,749 Nazarenes baptized across Haiti on the same day; over 1000 of these were baptized together at a district center. Similarly, in 1991, there were 1000 Korean Nazarenes baptized by their pastors in a mass gathering in Seoul. Sprinkling and pouring were the modes. The event attracted visiting district superintendents from Japan and India.[44]

---

[43] These incidents and numerous others are documented by Estep in "Baptismal Theology and Practice," pp. 47–52, 62. On M. E. Borders, see the *Journal* of the Chicago Central District, 1916: 24. On the baptism of thirty people, see the *Journal* of the Michigan District, 1945: 53.

[44] Regarding Schmelzenbach, see Estep, "Baptismal Theology and Practice," pp. 46–47. On mass baptisms in China, see *The Other Sheep* (August 1925): 6; ibid (August 1930): 6; and *Herald of Holiness* (Oct. 17, 1936): 36. On Haiti, see *Herald of Holiness* (Nov. 1, 1984): 35. On Korea, see *Grow* (Winter 1991): 1–4.

Home mission pastor J. B. Chapman baptizing believers in Durant, Oklahoma, around 1904. Chapman was later editor of *Herald of Holiness*, founding editor of *The Preacher's Magazine*, and from 1928 until his death in 1947, a general superintendent.

The early pluralism of baptismal practice generated a flow of questions to the editor of *Herald of Holiness,* the leading denominational paper, and this became an opportunity for instructing the church. In the 1920s, editor J. B. Chapman, an immersionist, defended infant baptism, immersion, and pluralism itself as acceptable and commendable practices of the church. When a reader demanded to know "what Biblical basis do Nazarenes have for baptizing babies," Chapman replied: "The innocent baby, being covered by the covenant of grace, is entitled to receive the symbol of that covenant … The meaning is just what is suggested—an outward sign of the child's inclusion in the covenant of grace." Chapman also counseled ministers to baptize by modes they did not prefer rather than make people wait for a minister in wholehearted agreement with their mode of choice. One thing he did *not* defend was the membership of unbaptized Christians in the Church of the Nazarene. He insisted: "It is expected that people who unite with the Church of the Nazarene shall have *some* water by *some* mode."[45]

Another person to recall is Mary Lee Cagle, who once stood steadfast for pouring as the only scriptural mode of baptism. After 1904, she embraced thoroughly the ideal of liberty on baptismal mode and timing, becoming on this issue a model pastor who was responsive to the individual consciences among her people. In an autobiography, she recounted a

---

[45] *Herald of Holiness* (Dec. 13, 1922): 2; (Aug. 2, 1922): 2; (Jan. 10, 1923): 3; (Feb. 7, 1923): 3. The direct quote is from the issue of Nov. 5, 1945, p. 8.

community baptismal service performed by her and her husband in an unchurched town in New Mexico. There were unbaptized people present who had been converted in various revivals over the years. Her account is written in the third person but refers to her husband and herself: "It was one time they baptized every way under the sun–by every mode possible. They dipped–they plunged–they poured–they sprinkled and they baptized babies. It was a time of rejoicing; and the shouts of the redeemed echoed and re-echoed through the hills."[46]

---

[46] Mary Lee Cagle, *Life and Work of Mary Lee Cagle* (Kansas City: Nazarene Publishing House, 1928), p. 119.

Chapter 3
Ministering to the Body, Not Just the Spirit:
Stages of Nazarene Social Ministry

A new era of Nazarene social ministries was initiated in the 1970s as a younger and hipper generation of pastors pioneered new urban ministries with significant social dimensions. Tom Nees left his pastorate at First Church of the Nazarene in Washington, D.C., to launch a new ministry in the city's riot corridor. Nees developed the Community of Hope by connecting with Gordon Cosby's Church of the Saviour and its Jubilee Housing ministry, and utilizing Cosby's philosophy of "mission groups." Community of Hope became a model for a new home mission movement and inspired other Nazarene urban ministries that embraced distinct social dimensions.[1]

In New York City, Paul Moore initiated a ministry in Times Square that embraced urban life and people. Moore's work combined two special emphases: outreach to the "down and out" transients who wandered through New York City, coupled with an intention to embrace the visual, musical, and stage arts—along with the people who made their livings in those professions.[2]

Moore took his crusade on the road by touring America with Manhattan Project, a musical group, and New York Christian Theater Company, an acting troupe. Nees promoted a new understanding of ministry through frequent appearances at Nazarene colleges and seminaries and in *The Mission Journal,* a monthly publication in which he shared the philosophy and experiences that characterized the new shape of his contemporary urban ministry. Nees and Moore directly inspired other urban ministers, among them Charlie Rizzo, Michael Christensen, Joe Colaizzi, Oliver Phillips, Bryan Stone, Dean Cowles, and John Hay, Jr., among others.

---

[1] Tom Nees, "Tribute to Gordon Cosby—A Servant Leader," Leading to Serve, January 6, 2009, http://leadingtoserve.com/?p=96

[2] See Paul Moore and Joe Musser, *Shepherd of Times Square* (Nashville & New York: Thomas Nelson Publishers, 1979).

New forms of urban ministry also took hold on the West Coast. The leaders of Los Angeles First Church of the Nazarene responded to the challenges of the varied urban landscape by embracing multi-congregationalism. By 1976, Los Angeles First Church had brought together on one campus Hispanic, Korean, and Anglo congregations. A Filipino congregation was soon added. First Church's approach respected ethnic subcultures, and the congregation sought to be socially responsible. The united congregations sponsored a school for neighborhood children that brought the different races together. Under pastor Ron Benefiel, the Bresee Institute for Urban Ministry was founded to train students in urban ministry philosophy and practice. Benefiel was joined at the Bresee Institute by Fletcher Tink, Michael Mata, and Jeff Carr.[3]

The new urban ministers found their inspiration primarily through a fresh understanding of the Scriptures and took note of the urban dynamics behind the rise and spread of early Christianity. But they also embraced precedents in earlier Christian history to counter a conservative notion that they were renegades who might lead the church to abandon its Pietist roots and embrace a liberal "social gospel." The fundamentalist/modernist controversy of the early and mid-twentieth century had fostered such stereotypical thinking among Evangelicals, who largely regarded American Christianity as consisting of two groups: Evangelicals who preached "a straight Gospel" of salvation, and liberal churchmen who knew nothing of "the real Gospel" and preached a "social gospel" as a thin substitute.

Nees and other new urban ministers knew that social ministry had a long and proud Evangelical heritage, and that historic Pietism had emphasized, not disdained, social concern. They found ample precedent for the shape of their own ministries in the examples of John Wesley, B. T. Roberts, and Phineas Bresee. Linking hands with the past, they drew upon a heritage of concern for the poor that characterized early Methodism, the Holiness Movement, and the early Church of the Nazarene.

In the process, they propagated a myth. They regarded their work as renewing the Church of the Nazarene's commitment to social ministries after a half-century of dormancy and neglect. In their understanding at the time, the Nazarenes had possessed an early commitment to social ministry that was abandoned in the 1920s with only a few exceptions. In this belief, they were as wrong as the conservatives who feared that the new social

---

[3] See Neil B. Wiseman, ed., *To the City with Love: A Source Book of Nazarene Urban Ministry* (Kansas City: Beacon Hill Press of Kansas City, 1976), pp. 52–56. This book as a whole provides today's reader with a basic overview of the shape of cutting-edge Nazarene urban ministry in mid-1970s America.

ministries might herald an unprecedented departure that could erode the denomination's commitment to traditional forms of ministry.

In truth, the Church of the Nazarene's commitment to social ministry had never died or become dormant. The social ministry vein was deeper and more interwoven with Nazarene life than conservatives or the new urban ministers recognized at the time. The new urban ministers were truly on the cusp of Nazarene social ministry's next major transformation, but they were initiating its third stage of development, not merely its second, as they imagined.

AT THE BEGINNING

The first Nazarenes generated a continual stream of new social ministries. The Southwest, especially, was fertile ground for such experiments. Orphanages, maternity homes, and urban rescue missions emerged as the three primary forms of social ministry among early Nazarenes.

Rest Cottage maternity home superintendents, staff, and unwed mothers.

The examples abound. Evangelist Oscar Hudson and wife operated an orphanage at their home in Lamasco, Texas, for several years before transferring the children to the Peniel Orphanage, on whose behalf they faithfully raised funds in their subsequent revival work.[4] J. F. Spruce and wife provided a home in Texas for a number of orphans.[5] Rev. Johnny Hill Jernigan worked for several years on behalf of the maternity home at Pilot Point Rest Cottage.

This, in turn prepared her to lead the Nazarene Home for unwed mothers in Bethany, Oklahoma, shortly after her family moved there in 1908. H. D. Brown, the first district superintendent appointed in the Church of the Nazarene, helped to establish orphan and maternity homes in the Pacific Northwest. Rev. Santos Elizondo founded an orphanage in Juarez, Mexico, soon after moving there to build a church among her people. She was

---

[4] *Pentecostal Messenger* (Feb. 1913): 4. For an account of Hudson's earlier role in establishing an orphans' home in Pilot Point that was later moved to Peniel, see his autobiography, *This I Remember: True Incidents of Pioneer Days* (Kansas City: Beacon Hill Press, 1965), pp. 39–45.

[5] Elizabeth Woolsey Spruce, "The Story of My Family," an edited transcript of oral history interviews, pp. 71-73.

caring for 40 orphans when she died many years later.⁶ At different times before 1920, maternity homes existed on the Abilene, Arkansas, Dallas, Kansas City, Louisiana, Oklahoma, San Francisco, Southern California, and Tennessee Districts, while Nazarene orphanages could be found in India, Mexico, and Texas.

Most were short-lived, rarely outlasting their founder. Most existed for a decade or less. Still, their short lives testify to the humanitarian impulse that the Nazarene founders associated with the call to holy living. As general superintendent John Goodwin wrote in 1920:

> Pure religion always has and always will have its two sides, purity and service. To neglect service in the welfare of others is to demonstrate a lack of purity. Holiness people should be preeminent in social service. This is what chiefly characterized the Early Church—their untiring service to bless their fellowmen and care for their widows and fatherless children.⁷

The Church of the Nazarene's 1923 *Yearbook* described the denomination's two general areas of social work—orphanages and maternity homes—and the five specific institutions that received a degree of general denominational support beyond the district level.⁸ These were the General Orphanage Board, created in 1919 by the Fifth General Assembly to foster interest in orphanages; the Orphans' Home in Peniel, Texas; and maternity homes for unwed girls and women: the Bethany Training Home in Memphis, Tennessee; Rest Cottage in Kansas City, Missouri; and Rest Cottage in Pilot Point, Texas.⁹

But the public face of Nazarene social ministry was on the verge of changing. Later that year, the Sixth General Assembly voted to "abandon the plan for a general orphanage, and it was recommended that the General Orphanage Board be dissolved, and the property of this Home be transferred back to the Districts of the Southern Educational District

---

⁶ *The Other Sheep* (May 1941): 5.
⁷ John W. Goodwin, "Holiness Children," *Herald of Holiness* (Nov. 10, 1920).
⁸ The Church of the Nazarene published yearbooks in 1923, 1924, and 1925, containing articles on each college, General Board department, and major ministry. The only known copies are in the Office of the General Secretary Collection, Nazarene Archives. Microfilm copies can be found in the Nazarene Documentary Sources microfilm project, owned by several Nazarene college libraries.
⁹ Rev. E. J. Fleming, ed., *Yearbook—Church of the Nazarene—1923* (Kansas City: Nazarene Publishing House, 1923), pp. 18–22, 27.

for its conduct and support."[10] Without general church support, the orphanage struggled on until closing in 1928. Bethany Training Home had also disappeared by 1925.[11] These events underscored the transient nature of early Nazarene social ministries.

Social Ministry and the Stages of Nazarene History

The short lives of the early social ministries testify to the fact that such ministry can never be separated from the denomination's larger story. The tides that ebb and flow generally in Nazarene life also shape the context of its social ministry. This is seen vividly in a basic aspect of these early Nazarene social ministries, namely their predominant character as "family enterprises"—a pattern that paralleled the early denomination's quest to establish secure institutional and financial footings.

To understand better the church's social ministry story, one must identify its hinges and inquire how compassionate ministries relate to the larger story of the Nazarenes. Historically, Nazarene social ministries have moved through three overlapping stages.

The "family enterprise" stage dominated until 1925 or so. A specific person or family generally initiated a new social ministry and stood behind it. The Rest Cottage maternity home at Pilot Point, Texas, was a prime example. It was founded by James P. Roberts in 1902. After his death, his brother and sister-in-law—John F. and Grace Roberts—took over as superintendents. When John F. Roberts died, leadership of the ministry passed to Geren Roberts, a member of the family's next generation, who served as Rest Cottage's superintendent until he retired in the mid-1970s. The home closed when he retired. It was the longest-lived Nazarene social ministry on American soil, but without two generations of leadership from the Roberts family it probably would not have endured as long as it did.

The second stage occurred when the first social ministries were successfully institutionalized within the framework of the general church. This phase began in the 1920s, when medical ministries were permanently incorporated into the church's cross-cultural missions program. This development preserved a continuous thread of Nazarene social ministry from the era of the founders down to the present. This phase was initiated by the building of teaching hospitals in China, Swaziland, and India in the 1920s and '30s. And it was represented in North America by the Samaritan Hospital and School of Nursing founded by Dr. Thomas E. Mangum in Nampa, Idaho.

---

[10] Ibid., 41.
[11] Ibid., 37-41.

The third stage was a more comprehensive institutionalization of social ministries beginning in the 1980s. This stage is represented by the development of three distinct but interacting agencies: Nazarene Compassionate Ministries International, Nazarene Compassionate Ministries USA/Canada, and a funding entity named Nazarene Compassionate Ministries, Inc. Along with this trio of umbrella organizations, the third stage has witnessed a proliferation of district and congregation-based social ministries in the United States and Canada and around the world.

Do these phases correspond to distinct periods in the larger Nazarene story? Historians do not necessarily agree with one another on how to periodize Nazarene history, but here is one scheme.

Period 1*: The Search for Foundations, 1887–1911*. This period was dominated by the story of the parent churches and the union movement that united them into a larger whole. It was an era in which social ministries flourished on the "family enterprise" model.

Period 2*: Consolidation and Institutionalization, 1911–1928*. In the second period of Nazarene history, a central publishing house and paper were authorized, a missionary society and youth auxiliary were organized, and the General Board and general budget were created in 1923. An increasingly sophisticated world mission strategy developed, and medical missions became an integral part of that system. The "family enterprise" model for social ministries was strong at the beginning of this period but dying by its end.

Period 3*: The Era of Frustration, 1928–1945*. Financial distress and world war thwarted the church's high ambitions and restricted its progress. Lack of money led to the policy of "retrenchment" as missionaries were called home and a number of missions were closed around the world. Medical ministries in Asia and Africa remained largely intact and, with rare exceptions, constituted the denomination's sole social ministries during this era of restricted opportunity.

Period 4*: The Era of Evangelism, 1945–1976*. The pent-up frustrations of the previous twenty years were released during the denomination's rapid expansion after World War II. The war economy had filled the church's treasury, and plans to enter new fields were realized. The Mid-Century Crusade for Souls at the beginning of this period is an apt symbol of the period as a whole. Medical ministries in Asia and Africa were joined by the addition of a Nazarene hospital in Papua New Guinea.

Period 5*: The Era of Internationalization, 1976–present*. The concept of an international church was embraced in the late 1970s. The rediscovery of the theological significance of the city and a new rebirth of compassionate ministries in North America and around the world are over-arching themes of this period.

Within this larger context, the historian faces a set of inter-related questions pertaining to the years 1925 to 1970. Why did the proliferation of compassionate ministries on the "family enterprise" model cease in the 1920s when so many new ones had emerged in the preceding decades? Why was the institutionalization of Nazarene social ministry in the 1920s limited to medical work and not institutionalized in a broader and more comprehensive form? And why did that pattern of "limited institutionalization," focused solely on medical work, persist decade after decade, well into the Era of Internationalization, without further expansion?

The Rise of Institutionalized Medical Work

The institutionalization of Nazarene medical missions provides clues for answering some of these questions. Nazarene missions in Asia and Africa possessed medical components nearly from the beginning. Medical field work was preeminent, but clinics and dispensaries appeared early on. Like the "family enterprise" social ministry, the advent of teaching hospitals in the 1920s began through the auspices of key persons and families, who made the building of these hospitals possible through their financial gifts and personal initiatives. After the hospitals were built, however, the general church assumed responsibility for their operation and maintenance.

Bresee Memorial Hospital. Bresee Memorial Hospital in China grew out of the personal vision of Rev. Clarence J. Kinne, a one-time Methodist minister who united with Phineas F. Bresee's work in Southern California in 1904. In response to Bresee's appeal, Kinne became manager of the Nazarene Publishing Company of Los Angeles at a fifty-percent cut in salary. There he was involved in publishing the *Nazarene Messenger,* a weekly edited by Bresee; the first Nazarene song-book, *Waves of Glory* (1905); and, after 1907, Sunday school curriculum. In 1911, the Third General Assembly called on the regional publishing houses to combine their assets and operations into a single, central publishing entity. Kinne, elected to manage the new enterprise, moved to Kansas City later that year. H. Orton Wiley summarized his role:

> To Brother Kinne fell the task of establishing a new publishing house. It was a difficult task. He formed the organization, purchased the equipment and carried on

the work of publication under the pressure of limited finances. He did his work well, and to him the church is indebted for the firm foundations which were laid.

Kinne resigned a few years later and returned to the West Coast.[12] He was well acquainted with many of the obstacles to establishing new institutions by the time he faced the challenge of building a hospital in China.

As early as 1913, Kinne indicated to missionary Peter Kiehn his strong interest in developing a credible Nazarene medical work in China. Kiehn later recalled that C. J. Kinne spent several years in self-education about medical missions before ever broaching the subject with the church's General Missionary Board. Kinne served the Southern California District as district missionary evangelist during his first two years back on the West Coast. In this capacity he preached throughout the district, organized classes for the study of mission literature, and preached and lectured on mission themes. He was not confined to Southern California but traveled up and down the Pacific coast, developing a base constituency to which he could turn when he founded the Nazarene Medical Missionary Union in 1921 to advance the idea of medical missions. Among its stated aims was the ambition to establish hospitals "under the direction of the General Missionary Board."

Kinne visited China for the first time in 1923. He examined hospitals operated by the mission boards of other denominations and selected a location for a new hospital: Tamingfu—already a headquarters location for the Nazarene work in northern China. After a brief visit to America to secure funds, Kinne returned to China in 1924 to build the hospital in earnest, serving as the on-site construction supervisor.[13]

Local wars hindered progress. The single year that Kinne had personally budgeted for the project lengthened into a longer time-span. Financial problems also arose. The hospital's main part was completed by 1925 and opened in October with 100 beds, but work on the rest of the hospital ground to a halt. Meanwhile, Kinne's wife died in California in 1926, while he was still in China.[14]

---

[12] *Herald of Holiness* (Nov. 16, 1932): 17–18.
[13] Peter Kiehn, "Rev. Clarence J. Kinne, a Missionary," *Other Sheep* (August 1933): 11.
[14] "Mrs. C. J. Kinne Joins Heavenly Host," *Herald of Holiness* (Feb. 10, 1926): 20; *Herald of Holiness* (Nov. 16, 1932): 17; and L. C. Osborn, *The China Story* (Kansas City: Nazarene Publishing House, 1969), pp. 42–45.

Bresee Memorial Hospital, Tamingfu, China.

Bresee Memorial Hospital was the only hospital in a city of some 14,000 residents, but Kinne estimated that the population base it was destined to serve could grow as high as two million people. He was determined to complete the job and returned to America to raise more funds. While there, he married Sue Bresee in 1927. She was the daughter of the late general superintendent and a long-time family friend. She accompanied him to China the following year. Kinne returned to Tamingfu to find that missionary nurse Mary Pannell had initiated a program for training Chinese nurses in his absence. Kinne resumed the role of construction supervisor and also consented to serve as pastor of the missionary force congregated in Tamingfu. Clarence and Sue Kinne remained in Tamingfu until 1930. They returned to California, leaving behind a fully constructed and equipped hospital.[15]

Bresee Memorial Hospital became the setting where dedicated physicians—including R. G. Fitz, Charles West, Hester Hayne, and Henry Wesche—worked with Chinese doctors, Chinese nurses, and missionary nurses, united by a common purpose to heal the sick. In the late 1930s, missionary accountant Catherine Flagler estimated that one-third of the budget spent on Nazarenes missions in China supported the hospital at Tamingfu and the outlying field and clinic work associated with it.[16]

---

[15] Kiehn, op.cit.; and *Herald of Holiness* (Nov. 16, 1932): 17; and *Yearbook*, 1925, p. 25.
[16] L. A. Reed and H. A. Wiese, *The Challenge of China* (Kansas City: Nazarene Publishing House, 1937), p. 85.

Raleigh Fitkin Memorial Hospital. Just as C. J. Kinne is linked indelibly with Bresee Memorial Hospital, so the names of Abram and Susan Fitkin—and their young son, Raleigh Fitkin—are linked to the Nazarene hospital built in Swaziland. So, too, are the names of David and Kanema Hynd.

Susan Fitkin's background was in the holiness revival wing of the Society of Friends. She and Abram became holiness evangelists and united with the Association of Pentecostal Churches of America in the 1890s, where she worked closely with Hiram F. Reynolds to support home and foreign missions. Abram left evangelistic work to become a Wall Street businessman and ascended to the highest rungs of secular success. Susan remained true to her early vision and vocation. She was a key founder of the Woman's Missionary Society in 1915 and served as its first president until 1948.

The early leader of Nazarene missions in Africa, Harmon Schmelzenbach, wanted to see medical work there from the beginning. The General Missionary Board's resources, however, were allocated to evangelism. Funds to finance Schmelzenbach's idea were not forthcoming until a tragedy occurred in the Fitkin family—the death of ten-year-old Raleigh Fitkin during surgery in 1914. As Susan's biographer expressed it, "here began a longing in his parents' heart to do something tangible" in Raleigh's memory. And tangible it was: first, a hospital in Swaziland; later over one million dollars to build and endow a children's wing at Yale University's hospital; and a half-million dollars to establish Raleigh Fitkin-Paul Morgan Memorial Hospital in Asbury, New Jersey, in memory of Raleigh and the son of
one of Abram's business partners.[17]

The first hospital that the Fitkins financed in Swaziland was small, located at Pigg's Peak, where there were other missionary interests. Construction began in 1919 and was completed the following year. The hospital had 18 beds and was placed under the direction of Lillian Cole, a nurse. Charles West, an American physician, arrived to serve there in 1921, but West's medical credentials were never accepted by the British authorities in the jurisdiction. The mission board finally sent him on to China in 1925 to serve at Bresee Memorial Hospital.

The original hospital in Swaziland faced another problem: it was located in an area of low population. The missionaries urged a larger

---

[17] Basil Miller, *Susan N. Fitkin: For God and Missions* (Kansas City: Nazarene Publishing House, n.d. [circa 1952]), p. 162.

hospital in a more populous area and received the support of Rev. George Sharpe, the missionary superintendent of Africa. In 1925, the Swazi government donated a tract of land for that purpose at Bremersdorp (now Manzini). It was situated on a major road leading from the Swazi capital. The Fitkins, with Mrs. Ada Bresee, were primary donors to the project. Sharpe's son-in-law, Scottish surgeon David Hynd, supervised construction of the new hospital. The Hynds had earned impeccable credentials. David was a native of Perth, Scotland, and a veteran of World War I. His medical training included degrees from the University of Glasgow, followed by post-doctoral training at the Royal College of Medicine in London. Nema Hynd was a nurse.

David Hynd, a surgeon, was Raleigh Fitkin Memorial Hospital's founder and chief administrator and the founder of the Red Cross in Swaziland.

They had received theological training and were ordained to the ministry together by general superintendent John Goodwin in 1924. Like Kinne, Hynd learned basic construction principles and methods from manuals, then taught them to others. The hospital was completed and dedicated in 1927. With Raleigh Fitkin Memorial Hospital as its hub, other Nazarene interests were located in Manzini, which developed into the effective headquarters of the Nazarene mission in Africa.[18]

The hospital's subsequent history was interwoven with Hynd's determined personality. A training program for nurses began in 1928, and other developments followed. Under Hynd's long tenure the hospital added "a children's ward, maternity ward, male and female medical and surgical wards, X-ray equipment, and a modern sanitary system."[19] By his retirement, the hospital had grown to 220 beds. He also branched out in other directions. He took the lead role in founding the Red Cross of Swaziland in 1932. Elizabeth Cole, assigned originally to the hospital in 1935 and later to field nursing, had a strong interest in working among patients with leprosy. Through her efforts and Hynd's, the government established a leper colony 40 miles from Manzini that RFM Hospital

[18] J. Fred Parker, *Mission to the World: A History of Missions in the Church of the Nazarene through 1985* (Kansas City: Nazarene Publishing House, 1988), pp. 123–28.
[19] Parker, *Mission to the World*, p. 130.

operated as an extension of its own work. Called Mbuluzi Leper Hospital, Cole was the resident nurse there from 1948 on. Hynd's devotion to his craft and to the Swazis was widely recognized and appreciated. During the British royal family's tour of Africa in 1947, King George VI personally awarded Hynd the honor of Commander of the British Empire in a special ceremony, with Princess Elizabeth, the future Queen, looking on. After they retired, David and Nema Hynd moved to the Leper Hospital, where they lived for several years.[20]

Thomas Mangum and the Samaritan Hospital. Thomas E. Mangum developed another link in the growing Nazarene investment in medical work. A Texan, his interest in medical missions was stimulated partly by his sister, Myrtle Mangum, an early missionary in India. In 1917, Northwest Nazarene College added a Department of Medical Missions and First Aid Instruction. The following year, President H. Orton Wiley encouraged Mangum to move to Nampa, Idaho, and build a facility adjacent to the college. Mangum had twin goals: to train nurses for mission service overseas and to provide health services to missionaries on furlough. Mangum opened the hospital in 1920 in a house he adapted to his purposes. Its early name was the Nazarene Missionary Sanitarium, emphasizing its role in providing physical and mental therapy to missionaries. A 50-bed hospital was constructed in stages and completed in 1933. The college transferred the hospital training program to the Sanitarium, and the first class of nurses graduated from it in 1931. In subsequent years, Mangum's enterprise became the Samaritan Hospital and School of Nursing. It trained many nurses who were assigned to medical ministries abroad by the Church of the Nazarene's Department of Foreign of Missions.[21]

Reynolds Memorial Hospital. By 1930, Nazarenes had made major investments in the construction and operation of hospitals on two continents and operated a smaller hospital on a third. In the 1930s, the church's fourth hospital was constructed: Reynolds Memorial Hospital in Washim, India. This occurred despite the financial hardships imposed on the denomination by the North Dakota Land Deal of the 1920s, which tied up church monies, and by the Great Depression.

Nazarene missionaries in India had discussed the need for a hospital for many years. The way was finally opened in 1935, when the Methodist Episcopal Church transferred property and ministries in Basim (now called

---

[20] William C. Esselstyn, *Nazarene Missions in South Africa* (Kansas City: Nazarene Publishing House, 1952), pp. 60–61.
[21] A summary is found in Parker, *Mission to the World*, pp. 90–92. For a biography of Mangum, see L. Alline Swann, *Song in the Night: The Story of Dr. and Mrs. Thomas E. Mangum* (Kansas City: Beacon Hill Press, 1957).

Washim), India, to the Church of the Nazarene, which quickly adapted two of the buildings to meet the needs of medicine and ministerial education. Dr. Orpha Speicher arrived at Basim in 1936 to head the medical work. The building designated for the hospital had been a classroom building, and Speicher found it insufficient in its existing form. She spent months adapting it to medical purposes. In the meantime, she studied the local language, conducted mobile clinics in nearby areas, and served as an "on call" doctor, seeing patients at the compound and making house calls. A hospital for women and children opened in 1938. As the number of patients increased, so did the demand for more space. Speicher oversaw the hospital's physical expansion. Like Kinne and Hynd, she became both architect and construction manager of the new additions, supervising each stage of their development. The Japanese incursion into Burma created new problems for British and American missionaries in adjacent India. The India Nazarene Mission Council decided that only a handful of Nazarene missionaries would remain, and Speicher and others returned to their native countries in 1942. For two years, the hospital operated at reduced capacity under the direction of Dr. Bower, a female Indian physician. Speicher returned to Basim in 1944, and Reynolds Memorial instituted a nurses' training program in 1947 under Jean Darling's direction. Other medical personnel joined the staff. Dr. Evelyn Witthoff and nurse Geraldine Chappell had been sent by the Nazarene mission board in 1942 but were intercepted en route and interred by the Japanese in a prison camp in the Philippines for the war's duration. After their liberation, they returned to America for physical rehabilitation before heading again to Asia and finally arriving at Reynolds Memorial Hospital in 1946. Speicher directed the construction of men's and surgical wings for the hospital. Like the hospitals in China and Swaziland, Reynolds Memorial developed into a hub for a wider-reaching medical ministry. Witthoff supervised the medical extension program as dispensaries were established in three other cities, and Reynolds Memorial personnel staffed rotating clinics at numerous villages and towns. Speicher remained in India until 1976, when Dr. Kamalakar Meshramkar succeeded her as the hospital's chief administrator.[22]

Later Medical Work. World War II forced Bresee Memorial Hospital to close in 1941, and the ascendancy to power of Mao's Red Army prevented Nazarenes from re-opening it ever again. But other hospitals were added to the denomination's work during the post-war era.

---

[22] Parker, *Mission to the World*, pp. 232, 237–38. And *India Nazarene Mission Council, New India and the Gospel* (Kansas City: Nazarene Publishing House, 1954), pp. 79–85.

The International Holiness Mission, a British denomination, focused its mission work in South Africa, where medical dispensaries were a part of its outreach program from the outset in 1911. One dispensary developed into a 66-bed hospital located first in Cottondale, and then, after 1937, in Acornhoek, South Africa. It was known as the Ethel Lucas Memorial Hospital and, along with six satellite dispensaries, it became a Nazarene ministry when the IHM merged with the Church of the Nazarene in 1952.[23]

Then, in the 1960s, the Nazarene World Missionary Society made the building of a hospital in Papua New Guinea the primary focus of its 50th anniversary year. Ken Dodd, a building contractor, began developing the physical plant at Kudjip in 1965, while Dr. Dudley Powers established the medical staff and processes. Dr. Evelyn Ramsey's association with the hospital began in 1969. She led the Kudjip Hospital for many years, while also working with others to create a concordance of the local Pidgen language. Eventually the wider story of Nazarene medicine in Papua New Guinea included the development of community-based medical services to serve rural areas. [24]

Each Nazarene hospital outside the United States became the hub of a larger network of medical healing that included smaller clinics and a network of field nurses whose ministries reached deep into the countryside. From 1930 on, medical missions involved a major portion of the budget dedicated to the church's wider missionary role. Nazarene medicine was a part of the church's strategy for world evangelization, but it was also a critical component of Nazarene social ministry. Indeed, it was a social ministry established for the benefit of some of the earth's poorest and neediest people.

MOTIVATIONS FOR EARLY MEDICAL MINISTRIES
What were the driving forces behind the church's attention to medical ministries? Why, for instance, did a gospel preacher like Harmon Schmelzenbach see medical work as an asset to the church's presence in Africa? At its base, the motivations that Nazarene medical personnel articulated were not fundamentally different from those that drove other types of social ministry within the church: there was a need and the means to assist it.

F. C. Sutherland, a missionary to China, stated simply but emphatically that "missionaries believe in medical missions." He did not disavow the

---

[23] Parker, *Mission to the World*, pp. 162–69.
[24] Parker, *Mission to the World*, pp. 608–11.

connection between medical missions and evangelism. In fact, he provides several accounts where medical missions opened he door to evangelistic presentation of the gospel. But Sutherland did not feel that evangelism was the sole basis of medical missions. He noted that Peter Kiehn and his wife, the first Nazarene missionaries appointed to China, saw a need for a Nazarene hospital there at an early date. Sutherland elaborated:

> The missionary lives in the midst of disease and physical suffering. If he is not a physician, there is very little of it that he can alleviate. … It means much that the skilled missionary physician is at hand, equipped and willing to take care of the sick and suffering. … Medical work gives testimony that the mission is interested in the people to a very deep extent. The Good Samaritan not only rescued the man who had been assaulted by the robbers, but he poured oil and wine upon his wounds, bound them up, and found an inn for him where he could rest and recover."[25]

Sutherland was clear: evangelism is one justification for medical missions, and compassion is also a sufficient justification. Lillian Cole echoed the note of compassionate response when she wrote to readers of *Other Sheep* magazine in 1916: "We feel that we must have a hospital as soon as possible, properly furnished to supply the needs of these poor people, and we must have a doctor for this field as soon as someone can be secured. We have very many sad cases."[26] No evangelistic hook was mentioned. There were only "very many sad cases."

The editor of *Other Sheep* magazine also stressed the compassionate impulse in an editorial note that accompanied a floor plan of the proposed hospital in Swaziland. He noted:

> Some may question the wisdom of investing money in a hospital in Africa, arguing that, with our limited means, it would be advisable to invest our funds in workers who devote their entire time to preaching and evangelizing. Seemingly they forget that one of the great agencies employed by our Master while on earth was through

---

[25] F. C. Sutherland, *China Crisis* (Kansas City: Nazarene Publishing House, 1948), pp. 86–87. Also see the remainder of the chapter titled "Healing the Sick."
[26] Lillian Cole, "Pigg's Peak [Swaziland], Africa," *Other Sheep* (December 1916): 3.

> ministering to their physical needs, and surely we who have been enlightened and live in a country that enjoys the blessings not only of civilization, but the blessings of Christianity, should use every agency that can be used to reach those who live in great darkness; not only spiritual darkness, but in great darkness concerning the care of the body, which is the temple of the Holy Ghost.[27]

The Church of the Nazarene's turn to medical missions in the 1920s provides compelling evidence that the compassionate impulse was not dying within the church but was being redirected. The next question is: Why?

Reshaping the Nazarene Social Conscience
The Compassionate Impulse from 1925–1945. The refocusing of the Nazarene social conscience around medical missions was part of a larger transformation of Nazarene life occurring simultaneously. Looming over this transformation was the shadow of the senior general superintendent, Hiram F. Reynolds. While the early vision of Phineas Bresee centered largely around "building up centers of holy fire" in the great urban centers of America, the vision that Reynolds brought to the united church was that of world evangelization. He embodied one of the dominant impulses of late nineteenth-century American Protestantism. In 1898 Reynolds sent out the first missionaries of any Nazarene parent body in his capacity as mission secretary of the Association of Pentecostal Churches of America. He brought to the united church an ability to articulate a positive basis for worldwide missions and to organize and motivate people for carrying out that purpose. For much of his quarter-century as general superintendent, Reynolds simultaneously wore the hat of general missionary secretary.

Reynolds' vision of worldwide missions was widely shared within the church, even in Bresee's home base, where Southern Californians like Leslie Gay, C. J. Kinne, and Maye McReynolds were exemplary in missionary zeal. The church's mission-mindedness was augmented in 1915 by the accession of the Pentecostal Mission, headquartered in Nashville, bringing into the denomination new mission fields in the Caribbean, Central America, and South America. The institutionalization of the compassionate impulse around medical missions rather than orphanages or maternity homes reflected the priorities that the mania for cross-cultural missions was working in other ways throughout the whole denomination.

---
[27] *Other Sheep* (May 1917): 4.

The reprioritizing of Nazarene life around missions was also shaped by the growth of the premillenialist perspective within the church. The roots of the Protestant missionary enterprise of the nineteenth century largely were in postmillenialism, not premillenialism. But the growing premillenialist movement after 1875 brought a new urgency to the cause of missions. Harold Raser has provided a useful survey of millenial perspectives within the larger American holiness movement, but no detailed study has yet been published on the growth of premillenialism among Nazarenes since 1908.[28] Yet premillenialism clearly emerged as the dominant eschatological perspective among Nazarenes. Some of the most influential early Nazarene leaders shared this view, including B. F. Haynes, the church paper's first editor; C. W. Ruth, whose advocacy was pivotal in the union of regional churches that created the Church of the Nazarene; J. B. Chapman, an editor and general superintendent; and E. P. Ellyson, a general superintendent and founder of the Department of Church Schools. As premillenialism took root within the Church of the Nazarene, its general tendency was to strengthen the priority given to cross-cultural missions.

A third factor shaped the pattern of social ministry among Nazarenes from 1925 to 1945: the church's worsening financial situation. The North Dakota Land Deal was an unfortunate investment of denominational funds that placed them beyond immediate use for the second half of the 1920s. The Great Depression further tightened a financial noose around the church's neck. The policy of retrenchment that closed some mission stations and brought missionaries home from the field was a bitter blow for the church. The economic realities of the day made prioritizing a necessity.

All these factors worked to rechannel the compassionate impulse of Nazarenes into medicine as the critical area where the church would give attention to the bodies, as well as the spirits, of men and women.

The Compassionate Impulse after 1945. The Church of the Nazarene emerged from the war years of 1941–45 in better shape than it had entered them. The war had heated the American economy, and the denominational treasury was stronger by 1946 than it had ever been. Why did medical ministries remain the only type of institutionalized social work within the Nazarene family? Why was there no broadening out into new social ministries during this period?

There are several reasons. The New Deal had changed several features of American life by constructing social safety nets. To Nazarene leaders, the

---

[28] Harold Raser, "Views on Last Things in the American Holiness Movement," in H. Ray Dunning, ed., *The Second Coming: A Wesleyan Approach to the Doctrine of Last Things* (Kansas City: Beacon Hill Press of Kansas City, 1995), pp. 161–85.

most needy people now seemed to lie outside North America. Moreover, the church's self-understanding had been formed in the years before World War II. It knew itself to be a missionary church, ambitious in its yearnings and full of zeal to evangelize. As the financial frustrations that dominated the 1930s receded, the Nazarenes entered one of their most sustained periods of growth through the expansion of cross-cultural missions. World war had not obliterated the compassionate impulse. When general superintendent Hardy Powers and Australian district superintendent A. A. E. Berg first explored the prospect of opening a new mission field for the church in Papua New Guinea, a hospital was very much a part of their grand scheme.[29] The pattern of channeling the humanitarian impulse around medical work remained intact.

As time passed, another trait reinforced the existing pattern of social ministry: amnesia. The church gradually forgot about the broader pattern of social ministry that had characterized the era of its founders. Indeed, it even forgot that it was undertaking social ministry under the guise of medical work. In the church's own mind, the practice of medicine was not "a social ministry" but "missions." This was illustrated when some students and faculty at Nazarene Theological Seminary published a short-lived periodical, *The Epworth Pulpit,* during the 1977–78 school year in the interests of "evangelical social action." Former missionary Wanda Knox was one of the subscribers. Knox told the wife of one of the student publishers that she subscribed only to remain informed about the next heresy to divide the church![30] Knox, ironically, was one of the biggest supporters of the Nazarene hospital in Papua New Guinea.

This amnesia came with a price. A large number of young Nazarenes in the early post-war era wanted to minister in areas of Christian social service and left the Church of the Nazarene because it did not offer a broader range of opportunities. During the 1960s, Robert Pierce, a graduate of Pasadena College, a Nazarene school, fashioned World Vision into a strong parachurch ministry that combined evangelistic and social service objectives. World Vision was aided in its mission by the intelligent commentary of another ex-Nazarene, the Rev. Paul Rees, a noted pastor and expositor of Christian holiness, whose writings and sermons argued cogently that social ministries gave credibility to the Christian witness. John L. Peters, a product of Little Rock First Church of the Nazarene, a general Nazarene Young Peoples' Society president, a chaplain in the waning days of World War II, and a credible historian of the doctrine of

---

[29] Parker, *Mission to the World*, pp. 608–9.
[30] Knox made her statement to Nancy Leth, wife of *The Epworth Pulpit* editor, Carl Leth.

entire sanctification in Methodism, joined the Methodist Church in the 1950s to found World Neighbors, a ministry to the poor outside America's borders. His critique of the Nazarenes was that they lacked "a full-orbed Gospel." Paul McCleary, a graduate of Olivet Nazarene College, also left the Nazarene ranks and later served as executive director of Church World Services.[31]

While the basic shape of Nazarene social ministries in the post-war era continued down a path laid out in the 1920s, the foundations for a new consensus about Christian social ministry were being laid. The Nazarene historian Timothy L. Smith's *Revivalism and Social Reform* (1956) and *Called Unto Holiness* (1962) played roles in reminding Nazarenes about a broad tradition of social service that had characterized the broad evangelical tradition and the Church of the Nazarene in earlier years. Indeed, *Revivalism and Social Reform* was one of two or three instrumental texts that helped frame the argument for renewing evangelical social work generally, and it made Smith a leading evangelical thinker in his day.

Other roots lay outside the Nazarene door. The civil rights struggle of the 1960s shook the social complacency of Americans and reminded them of obligations yet unredeemed. Harvey Cox's *The Secular City* was not a staple on many Nazarene reading lists, but American evangelicals increasingly heard the prophet's call and began pondering anew the theological meaning of the city. This impulse also resonated throughout the whole Evangelical world. This was explicitly represented at the International Congress on World Evangelization, held in 1974 in Lausanne, Switzerland. The Lausanne Covenant, adopted by Evangelicals from around the world, stated clearly in clause 5, "Christian Social Responsibility," God's desire for social justice, noting that:

> The message of salvation implies also a message of judgment upon every form of alienation, oppression and discrimination, and we should not be afraid to denounce evil and injustice wherever they exist. When people receive Christ they are born into his kingdom

---

[31] Peters, McCleary, and Rees were all plenary speakers at the Church of the Nazarene's first Compassionate Ministries Conference in November 1985. Nearly 500 people attended the conference. See Albert L. Truesdale, Jr., and Steve Weber, eds., *Evangelism and Social Redemption: Addresses from a Conference on Compassionate Ministry*, November 1985 (Kansas City: Beacon Hill Press of Kansas City, 1987).

and must seek not only to exhibit but also to spread its righteousness in the midst of an unrighteous world.[32]

World Vision's growing popularity among evangelicals also played a major role in reshaping the Nazarene conscience. The Haiti famine in 1975 and the Guatemala earthquake in 1976 spurred the development of the Church of the Nazarene's Hunger and Disaster Fund. Meanwhile, also in Haiti, a young Nazarene missionary named Steve Weber was working among the poor in ministries that were preparing him to lead Nazarene Compassionate Ministries International a decade later.

The third and present phase of Nazarene social ministry was now in the offing. It would develop its primary character in the 1980s. That phase is marked by a broad range of compassionate ministries supported by churches and districts, and by a broader institutionalization of global social ministries coordinated through general church support, including new initiatives in hunger and disaster relief, child sponsorship, economic development, and ministry to those around the world with AIDS.

From the impulses of the 1960s and 1970s, the social ministry style of American Nazarenes and other evangelicals was refashioned and reborn.

---

[32] C. Rene Padilla, ed., *The New Face of Evangelicalism: An International Symposium on the Lausanne Covenant* (Downers Grove, Ill.: InterVarsity Press, 1976), p. 87, and see Athol Gill's exposition of clause 5, pp. 89–102. Also see: www.lausanne.org/covenant.

Chapter 4
Strange Bedfellows:
Nazarenes and Fundamentalism

"Every man in this body is a fundamentalist, and so far as we know there is not a modernist in the ranks of the Church of the Nazarene," declared general superintendent R. T. Williams to the assembled delegates and visitors to the church's Seventh General Assembly.[1] It was 1928, three years after the Scopes Trial in Tennessee, and it is doubtful that many in his audience disagreed.

Twenty-one years later, writing in *The Preacher's Magazine*, Oscar Reed, a young professor of philosophy and religion, argued that fundamentalism was wholly incompatible with Wesleyan theology. Using an argument made by many others, Reed asserted that Christian fundamentalism thrives in the soil of Calvinism. Since Calvinism is antithetical to Wesleyan-Arminian theology, Wesleyans cannot be fundamentalists without betraying their most cherished theological principles.[2]

So were the Nazarenes of the 1920s and beyond fundamentalists or not? The answer depends, largely, on how one assesses fundamentalism and views its function in American religion.

The year after R. T. Williams spoke, H. Richard Niebuhr framed the conflict between modernists and fundamentalists as one "between urban and rural religion." The fundamentalists, he said, "reflected not only the memories and habits of frontier faith but also the experiences

---

[1] Quadrennial Address of the Board of General Superintendents, *Journal of the Seventh General Assembly of the Church of the Nazarene* (Kansas City: Nazarene Publishing House, 1928): 58.

[2] Oscar F. Reed, "Definitive Statements Concerning Nine Philosophies of Religion," *The Preacher's Magazine* (March-April 1949): 12–13, and (May–June 1949): 11. A similar argument was used by Wes Tracy as editor of *Herald of Holiness* to answer the question, "Do Nazarenes belong in the Fundamentalist camp?" Tracy responded that "Nazarene thinkers have usually made careful distinctions between themselves and Fundamentalists. Nevertheless, many Nazarenes embrace the Fundamentalist ethos." "The Question Box," *Herald of Holiness* (Sept. 1998): 20.

of rural life." He predicted a happy but brief life for fundamentalism, since "rural religion ... is subject to further transition" as modernity encroaches on the countryside.³ The acerbic social critic, H. L. Mencken, was not so convinced and portrayed fundamentalists as ignorant yokels who inhabited and thrived in America's cities as well. "Heave an egg out of a Pullman window," he declared, "and you will hit a Fundamentalist almost anywhere in the United States today. They swarm in the country towns, inflamed by their pastors ... They are thick in the mean streets behind the gasworks. They are everywhere that learning is too heavy a burden for mortal minds."⁴ Norman Furniss, whose prose lacks Mencken's propensity toward sarcastic comment, examined fundamentalism far more thoroughly in *The Fundamentalist Controversy* (1954). He also regarded fundamentalists as largely uncultured.

Richard Hofstadter's classic work, *Anti-Intellectualism in American Life* (1963), viewed fundamentalists as deprived and argued that status or esteem was what they lacked and sought:

> The fundamentalist mind has had the bitter experience of being routed in the field of morals and censorship, on evolution and Prohibition, and it finds itself increasingly submerged in a world in which the great and respectable media of mass communication violate its sensibilities and otherwise ignore it. ... [I]t has been elbowed aside and made a figure of fun."

In their marginalization, fundamentalists were being driven by their desire *to be* somebody, Hofstadter argued. He noted their penchant for right-wing politics.⁵

Hofstadter did not mention fundamentalism in his celebrated essay, "The Paranoid Style in American Politics," but there were important suggestions there also. In that essay, he identified a style of politics characteristic of groups who are motivated by their deep belief in conspiracy theories. These groups fear that others—whether Deists, Freemasons, Roman Catholics, anarchists, or communists—are out to destroy their way of life. And in related essays, Hofstadter identified fundamentalists

---

³ H. Richard Niebuhr, *The Social Sources of Denominationalism* (Cleveland and New York: Meridian Books, 1957; reprinted from 1929 edition by Henry Holt & Company), pp. 184–86.
⁴ H. L. Mencken, "To Expose a Fool," *The American Mercury* (October 1925): 160.
⁵ Richard Hofstadter, *Anti-Intellectualism in American Life* (New York: Vintage Books, 1966), p. 134.

with this style of politics, characterizing them as people with "a Manichean view of the world" who see politics in terms of an eternal struggle between absolute good versus absolute evil.[6]

Other writers on fundamentalism have eschewed interpretations of economic, educational, or social deprivation, focusing, instead, on mood or attitude. Harry Emerson Fosdick, the renowned liberal preacher, provided a simple but useful definition of fundamentalism in his well-known sermon, "Shall the Fundamentalists Win?" Theological conservatives and fundamentalists can believe precisely the same doctrines, Fosdick stated. What separates the two is not the content of their doctrine but the basic spirit that the fundamentalist brings to it. Fundamentalism is not simply Christian orthodoxy; it is militant orthodoxy—orthodoxy on the warpath, with a glint of blood in its eye.[7]

This idea was endorsed by George Dollar of Bob Jones University. In his sympathetic treatment of his own movement, *A History of Fundamentalism in America* (1973), Dollar argued that fundamentalism is "the literal exposition of all the affirmations and attitudes of the Bible and the militant exposure of all non-Biblical affirmations and attitudes." Like Fosdick, Dollar regarded militancy as the key.[8]

Louis Gasper's *The Fundamentalist Movement, 1930–1956* (1963) took a different tack by treating fundamentalism as a Christian separatist movement whose reason for being rests in the distance it can gain and maintain from mainline churches. It is not just orthodoxy. To Gasper, the essence of fundamentalism is *sectarian* orthodoxy.

A similar view was adopted by Fuller Theological Seminary's E. J. Carnell—professor of apologetics, peer of Carl F. H. Henry, and leading figure in the post-war Evangelical renaissance. Carnell sought to differentiate American evangelicals from fundamentalists. He argued that fundamentalism claims to represent orthodox Christianity but actually enshrines a cultish view of it. He described the primary traits of this cultic

---

[6] Compare the essay "The Paranoid Style in American Politics" with an essay following it, "Pseudo-Conservatism Revisited," which does deal with Fundamentalists. In Richard Hofstadter, *The Paranoid Style in American Politics and Other Essays* (Cambridge: Harvard University Press, 1964).

[7] Fosdick preached: "We should not identify the Fundamentalists with the conservatives. All Fundamentalists are conservatives, but not all conservatives are Fundamentalists. The best conservatives can often give lessons to the liberals in true liberality of spirit, but the Fundamentalist program is essentially illiberal and intolerant." Specifically he identified a Fundamentalist as one whose "intention is to drive out of the evangelical churches men and women of liberal opinions."

[8] George Dollar, *A History of Fundamentalism in America* (Greenville, S.C.: Bob Jones University, 1973), xv.

orthodoxy: "mores and symbols of its own devising," detachment from "the church universal," and belligerence. By contrast, those rooted in classical Protestant Orthodoxy are "impatient with the small talk of the cult; they long for authentic conversation on historic themes" and tend to be better educated.[9] "The doctrine of the church is the dividing line between fundamentalism and [classical] orthodoxy, and the line is a sharp one," said Carnell. He narrowed in:

> Fundamentalism rests its case on a separatist view of the church. It contends that when a denomination has modernists among its clergy or missionaries, a Christian must withdraw financial support until said modernists are deposed. And if financial boycott fails, a Christian must disaffiliate forthwith; he must start a "pure witness" for the Gospel ...
>
> Fundamentalism [has] formulated its view of the church with an eye to the interests of the cult. Fundamentalists believe they are superior because they have withdrawn from historic denominations; they imagine that they alone glorify the gospel. Since the fundamentalist is deprived of the happy security that comes from communion with the church universal, he must devise substitute securities all his own. And the handiest substitute—the one calling for the least energy and skill—is to appear better by making others appear worse. In plain language, the fundamentalist tattles, because censure implies superiority.[10]

---

[9] Edward John Carnell, "Orthodoxy: Cultic vs. Classical," *The Christian Century* (March 30, 1960): 377.

[10] Ibid., p. 378. In a different article on the subject, Carnell argues that "Fundamentalism is a paradoxical position. It sees the heresy in untruth but not in unloveliness. If it has the most truth, it has the least grace, since it distrusts courtesy and diplomacy. ... Fundamentalism is a lonely position. It has cut itself off from the general stream of culture, philosophy, and ecclesiastical tradition. This accounts, in part, for its robust pride. Since it is no longer in union with the wisdom of the ages, it has no standard by which to judge its own religious pretense. It dismisses non-fundamentalistic efforts as empty, futile, or apostate. Its tests for Christian fellowship become so severe that divisions in the Church are considered a sign of virtue. And when there are no modernists from which to withdraw, fundamentalists compensate by withdrawing from one another. ... Status by negation must be maintained or the raison d'être of fundamentalism is lost." See Edward John Carnell, "Fundamentalism," in *A Handbook of Christian Theology*, eds. Marvin Halverson and Arthur A. Cohen (New York: Meridian Books, 1958), p. 143.

Elmer Towns, a Jerry Falwell associate and self-avowed fundamentalist, pushed the notion of fundamentalist separatism further, noting two types of fundamentalists. "First-degree" separatists refuse to have any direct fellowship with theological liberals but will fellowship with fellow conservatives who do. "Second-degree" separatists even avoid fellowship with other conservatives if they fellowship with liberals.[11] To illustrate what this means, a first degree separatist, it is said, will not fellowship with the mainline church folk whom Billy Graham fellowships with, but they will fellowship with Billy Graham. The second-degree fundamentalist will not even do that.

Ernest Sandeen's scholarship marked a sharp turn toward understanding fundamentalism primarily as a theological movement. His *Roots of Fundamentalism* (1970) was quickly recognized as a seminal work. Sandeen argued that fundamentalism flowed from the confluence of two separate streams in American religious thought: the nineteenth-century Princeton theology's doctrine of the Bible's inerrancy, and the growing grass-roots influence of dispensational premillenialism. Sandeen detailed each stream's emergence. He did not argue that these streams completely merged, or that a true fundamentalist must exhibit both traits. In fact, the "old Princeton" theology migrated from New Jersey to Philadelphia, to be newly enshrined at Westminister Theological Seminary, where even yet it retains a pristine flavor unaffected by popular premillenialism.

Other groups, such as the Churches of Christ, who would strike many people as fundamentalists, largely rejected the new premillenialism as well, at least until recently. The dispensationalist movement, on the other hand, thoroughly embraced the Princeton view of biblical inerrancy because that view bolstered its sense of authority, which dispensationalism's emphasis on predictive prophecy required. Thus a large popular following developed in American Christianity in which the two streams were blended. This popular following included nearly all Pentecostals, a large majority of white Baptists, many black Baptists, and more than a few Nazarenes and other Wesleyans. The seminal nature of Sandeen's work can be seen in subsequent studies of dispensationalism by Timothy Weber and various historians of early Pentecostalism, not to mention a new round of attention focused on the Princeton theologians.[12]

---

[11] Elmer L. Towns, "Trends Among Fundamentalists," *Christianity Today* (July 6, 1973): 12.
[12] For examples, see Timothy Weber, *Living in the Shadow of the Second Coming* (1983); Robert Mapes Anderson, *Vision of the Disinherited* (1979) which includes argument that Pentecostalism emerged primarily as a millennial movement with the "gifts of the Spirit" as evidences of Christ's soon return; Mark Noll, *The Princeton Theology* (1983), a source book

Sandeen's work was followed shortly by George Marsden's *Fundamentalism and American Culture* (1980), another seminal work. He brought both theological and sociological lenses to bear on the problem. He interpreted fundamentalists as religious conservatives who are profoundly conflicted by modernity. On one hand, they strenuously rejected the central tenets of twentieth-century biology, but not the medicine based on it. They decried the way others used technological advances to reach the masses, but adapted the same tools to their own purposes. They benefited from rising middle-class prosperity and social change, yet were threatened by the prospect of further change. Marsden predicted that fundamentalism will always be visible in the religious landscape since social change is ongoing and always engenders reaction among religious conservatives.

Like Sandeen, Marsden's chapter on "The Holiness Movement" identified the spread of dispensational premillenialism with this movement. Yet Wesleyans barely make an appearance in this chapter. Marsden's treatment of "the Holiness Movement" focuses instead on the Keswick-holiness movement, the English import disseminated across America by D. L. Moody, R. A. Torrey, and others in their circle. Perhaps this is telling. While fundamentalism made significant inroads into the life of Nazarenes and sister Wesleyan churches, the larger story of fundamentalism, ultimately, is not the central theme in their stories.

The literature on fundamentalism includes a sub-strain that deals with the fundamentalist tendency toward right-wing politics. Early works in this genre focused on fundamentalists who were on the extreme right. Ralph Lord Roy's *Apostles of Discord* (1953) examined fundamentalism's seamy side by looking at such polarizing personalities as the anti-Semitic evangelist Gerald Winrod, the reactionary Gerald L. K. Smith, publisher of the monthly *Cross and Flag,* who raged against Blacks, Jews, and the United Nations, and the anti-communist, anti-internationalist Carl McIntire, among others. Erling Jorstad's *The Politics of Doomsday* (1970) extended the story another twenty years, updating Roy's work to include Billy James Hargis, whose Christian Crusade reduced the historic faith to anti-communism, and others of his type. Roy stated clearly that "most fundamentalists ... do not share [these] racial and religious bigotries."[13] Not all of his readers remembered or may have believed that statement since fundamentalist hate speech was easy to find on the nation's radio waves during the 1950s and 1960s. And Nazarenes were not immune

---

with a fine introduction by the editor; and Brad Longfield, *The Presbyterian Controversy* (1993).

[13] Ralph Lord Roy, *Apostles of Discord* (Boston: The Beacon Press, 1953), p. 27.

from it. Shortly before the Nazarene Publishing House published Carl Bangs' *The Communist Encounter* (1963), Hargis blasted Bangs in a radio broadcast for statements Bangs made in a *Herald of Holiness* article.[14] After Bangs' book appeared, a group of California Nazarenes, calling themselves the Committee of Concerned Laymen, likewise attacked Bangs for not being sufficiently anti-communist and for commending the noted Christian social ethicist, John C. Bennett, whom they insinuated was a communist fellow-traveler.

Apart from the extremists, the more general conservative tendencies of fundamentalists were not studied as carefully until later, despite the fact that Southern white fundamentalism constituted one of the significant bastions of resistance to civil rights for Blacks. This changed with the growing interest in Southern religious history that emerged through Samuel S. Hill's influence in the mid-1970s, and the development late in that decade of "the new religious-political right." The latter became the subject of intense interest by the popular press and students of the social sciences—political scientists, historians, and sociologists alike. A large and growing literature on the political conservatism of rank and file fundamentalism has emerged since then.

THE EVANGELICAL KALEIDOSCOPE

My attitude toward the historiography of fundamentalism is straightforward. Each theory about it grabs some facet of the truth and tends to have value, but none is complete in itself. In particular, I find merit in Harry Emerson Fosdick's notion that fundamentalists are theological conservatives with militant (almost exclusive) attitudes, coupled with Carnell's notion of fundamentalism as sectarian separatism. Further, I have found it helpful to examine fundamentalism in light of a model for understanding American evangelicalism that Timothy Smith advanced.

Smith argued in the 1970s that American evangelicalism should be understood as a mosaic. Evangelicalism is not monolithic but embraces a wide range of different theological communities that often think quite different thoughts. Reformed evangelicals do not think or always act like Wesleyan evangelicals. Mennonite evangelicals differ in thought and ethics from Baptist evangelicals. Each religious community occupies a different place in the economy of American evangelicalism. Each is a different piece

---

[14] The attack on Bangs was the subject of Hargis' radio broadcast of October 1, 1962. Transcript in the "National Council of Churches—Evangelism Department" File, Nazarene Archives. Photocopy also in the Carl Bangs profile folder. Among other "sins," Bangs had quoted from *The Christian Century*, which Hargis called "the voice of religious apostasy." Bangs' article appeared in *Herald of Holiness* (August 22, 1962).

of theological stone within a larger mosaic. One must look at the whole mosaic, and one must also look at the individual parts.

After feedback and further reflection, Smith shifted his model. He recognized that American evangelicalism is not static but in a state of constant flux. Each of the distinct theological communities under the Evangelical tent is also in flux—shifting, turning, changing. As the pieces shift, so does the total picture. In light of this reflection, Smith retired the notion of an Evangelical mosaic and began speaking, instead, of the Evangelical kaleidoscope—the colorful picture that changes every second.[15]

The helpful notion of the Evangelical kaleidoscope can influence our notions of fundamentalism. If we grasp that there are a variety of ways a person or a community can be Evangelical, then it is no big leap to conclude that there also exist a variety of ways that they can be fundamentalist. Not all modes of fundamentalism should be regarded as alien to the Wesleyan tradition. Indeed, we can understand one type of Wesleyan fundamentalism as a commitment to the central doctrines of grace and holiness of the Wesleyan tradition, but coupled to a perspective shaped by disdain toward modernism or some aspect of it, such as modern science. Other forms of Wesleyan fundamentalism may be based on rigid legalism, or even around the form of arid apologetic Wesleyan theology that John Allan Knight dubbed "holiness scholasticism," or even as a marriage of two or more of these. These are stances one may dislike and can challenge as incompatible with the radical optimism of grace that is central to a Wesleyan understanding of life, grace, and faith. They can be critiqued as a violation of the Wesleyan ideal that holds together "those two so long disjoined, knowledge and vital piety." There they are, nonetheless.

I remember vividly a question that was asked when defending my doctoral dissertation many years ago. The examination was over a study of Mary Lee Cagle, the staunchest advocate of women's ordination and ministry in the early Church of the Nazarene. I was asked about her attitude toward fundamentalism and replied that she undoubtedly considered herself one. Eyebrows were immediately raised all around the table. An examiner then stated that Cagle was in the ironic position of championing women in ministry, but simultaneously identified with the very impulse that later choked it. I disputed that conclusion and have reflected on the conversation often since then. Mary Lee Cagle, like most of the Wesleyan women preachers of her generation, regarded herself as

---

[15] Timothy L. Smith, "The Evangelical Kaleidoscope and the Call to Christian Unity." *Christian Scholar's Review* 15 (1986): 125–40.

a fundamentalist and would not accept the notion, popular today, that "fundamentalist inroads" into Nazarene life precipitated the significant decline of women in her denomination's ministry after 1935. She almost certainly would say that if the church forgot the biblical basis for women in ministry, then it was because the church neglected its ongoing exegetical task and failed to meet its catechetical obligations, allowing doctrines of the ministry generated in other exegetical-theological traditions to fill the void. But as for her, Cagle's own fundamentalism merely strengthened her determination to show that the basis of her ministry was grounded firmly and irrevocably in the Christian Scriptures.

One can view the first wave of American fundamentalism as a phase in the history of American evangelicalism that deeply tinged all the pieces in the Evangelical kaleidoscope. Among theological conservatives, there were few corners where fundamentalism did not penetrate in the 1920s, 1930s, and 1940s. The Southern Baptist Convention suffered more than one split at the hands of those who thought the denomination was not nearly conservative enough. Pentecostals largely viewed themselves as fundamentalists at this time. Conservative Lutherans became more so. And R. T. Williams said, "Every man in this body is a fundamentalist, and so far as we know there is not a modernist in the ranks of the Church of the Nazarene." While it was not literally true that "every man" present was a fundamentalist—H. Orton Wiley, for instance, was very present and very clearly not one, nor were others present for the speech—still the seepage of fundamentalism was evident all around. It was, in fact, knee deep.

The Church of the Nazarene

The story of Evangelical Christianity's emergence from fundamentalism has been told many times. It is partly a story of joint effort across denominational lines, symbolized by the founding of *Christianity Today* and the National Association of Evangelicals as harbingers of a new style of post-fundamentalist evangelicalism. But it is equally the case that each denomination affected by fundamentalism later backed away from it by its own methods, each devising its own strategy for releasing fundamentalism's grip. H. Orton Wiley's actions at the 1928 General Assembly demonstrate this.

The move was on to introduce the notion of inerrancy into the church's Article of Faith on Scripture. Wiley had spent several years researching and writing the work that would be published eventually as his three-volume *Christian Theology*. Alert to the issues, and oriented to an Anglo-Methodist understanding of Scripture, he guided the General Assembly to amend the statement carefully. The revised article on Scripture adopted by the Nazarenes in 1928 read: "We believe in the plenary inspiration of the Holy Scriptures by which we understand the sixty-six books of the Old and New Testaments, given by divine inspiration, inerrantly revealing the will of God concerning us in all things necessary to our salvation; so that whatever is not contained therein is not to be enjoined as an article of faith."[16] Like the Church of England's corresponding article on Scripture that John Wesley and early British Methodists had been weaned on, and the corresponding article in American Methodism, with which Bresee, Reynolds, and other key Nazarene leaders were familiar, the revised Nazarene article on Scripture in 1928 emphasized the church's confession that Scripture is a reliable and trustworthy witness to salvation, while avoiding fundamentalism's more extreme emphasis. Wiley had succeeded in preventing the urge to tinker from drifting over into the Princeton notion of the total inerrancy of scripture, with its attendant problems.[17] By contrast, the Wesleyan Methodist Church went the opposite way in 1951, adopting the strictest view of inerrancy and creating a striking theological difference between it and its closest sister denominations—the Nazarenes and the Free Methodists.[18]

Nevertheless, in the conflict between fundamentalists and modernists, Nazarene sympathies were clearly on fundamentalism's side and against religious skepticism, the higher critics of the Bible, the Darwinists, and the liberal Protestant theologies. Indeed, there is abundant evidence that Nazarenes regarded liberal Protestantism as the unwelcome accommodation of Christianity to distinctly anti-Christian assumptions. In its opposition to theological modernism, the Church of the Nazarene underwent a fundamentalist phase, as did other evangelical denominations.

---

[16] "Articles of Religion" in *Encyclopedia of World Methodism*, Vol. 1 (Nashville: United Methodist Publishing House, 1974) provides the Anglican and Methodist creeds laid out in parallel fashion. See pp. 147–48 for the articles on Scripture. Church of the Nazarene, *Manual*, (Kansas City: Nazarene Publishing House, 1928), p. 22.

[17] Paul M. Bassett's fine study of this is in "The Theological Identity of the North American Holiness Movement: Its Understanding of the Nature and Role of the Bible," in Donald W. Dayton and Robert K. Johnston, eds. *The Variety of American Evangelicalism* (Knoxville: University of Tennessee Press, 1991), pp. 72–108. Also see Bassett's "The Fundamentalist Leavening of the Holiness Movement" *Wesleyan Theological Journal*, 13 (Spring 1978): 65–91.

[18] Ira Ford McLeister and Roy Stephen Nicholson, *Conscience and Commitment: The History of the Wesleyan Methodist Church of America* (Marion, Indiana: The Wesley Press, 1976), pp. 226–27. Stephen Paine, president of Houghton College, was the primary leader of this change. See Wayne E. Caldwell, ed., *Reformers and Revivalists: The History of the Wesleyan Church* (Indianapolis: The Wesley Press, 1992), p. 330.

Thus critical questions emerged as fundamentalism's conflict with modernism grew sharper. How extensively would fundamentalism alter the Nazarene self-understanding? Nazarenes had developed a distinct theological identity early in their history, blending Wesleyan ideas of grace, faith, and holiness, American Methodist ideas of polity, and several assumptions of the believers' church tradition. Would that unique identity remain intact as the fundamentalist crusade developed, or would it be lost, swallowed up by a growing affinity with a newer and broader twentieth-century movement whose spirit and purposes were quite different from those of the Wesleyan holiness movement that had birthed the Nazarenes?

The issue can be drawn even more clearly by considering the nature of movements. Movements share certain features, whether religious or social in nature. They are not bred by consensus; they are born of dissent. Lawrence Goodwyn's history of the populist movement of the late nineteenth century is a helpful place to start for understanding their character. In *The Populist Moment,* Goodwyn argues that any new movement begins because people analyze a particular set of conditions. That analysis must seem cogent, at least to some of the people affected. Spokesmen who believe the analysis must be recruited, or else the analysis goes nowhere. The spokesmen spread the ideas of the movement and recruit new believers. Since the establishment controls the press, a movement must generate its own publishing enterprise. Tracts, booklets, broadsheets and periodicals produced by the movement press assist in recruitment and help the movement consolidate its gains. Meetings and conventions rally the faithful and energize them. Goodwyn stresses the vital significance of a movement maintaining its focus. His thesis, highly provocative, is that populism began as an agrarian revolt that achieved nearly all the basic steps but failed to mature as a political movement when populists began sharing their platforms with the advocates of the free silver campaign. This muddied the agrarian message, altered populism's objectives, and led to the movement's rapid demise.[19]

Goodwyn's conclusion regarding populism's failure is still debated, but his understanding of a movement's stages is helpful. The Wesleyan holiness movement established its own analysis of mainline Protestantism, particularly Methodism. Movement leaders diagnosed the problem as decline within Methodism as they witnessed the erosion of loyalties to

---

[19] Lawrence Goodwyn, *The Populist Moment: A Short History of the Agrarian Revolt in America* (Oxford, London, and New York: Oxford University Press, 1978). *The Populist Moment* is a 342-page abridgment of a more comprehensive work, *Democratic Promise: The Populist Movement in America* (1976).

the class meeting and other mechanisms designed to foster Christian holiness. In response, they generated a reform movement that sought to recover Wesley's emphasis on Christian perfection. They offered spiritual solutions to what they regarded as growing spiritual laxity and doctrinal confusion over the theology of holiness. It is important to note that those who opposed Wesleyan holiness theology were also evangelicals, not liberals. Methodism's debate over holiness was a debate among evangelical Methodists. The Wesleyan holiness movement's critique of creeping formalism and the culture bred by growing middle-class prosperity was developed before Darwin and before the higher critics of the Bible. The Holiness Movement used evangelists as its spokesmen, and developed a press that was independent of the Methodist officials. Two generations of leadership successfully kept it within the fold of mainline Methodism, but the movement's third generation became radically diverse and with that diversity came the rise of the holiness churches. As the movement fractured, the holiness churches that emerged viewed themselves as faithful to the original ideals of the movement and as new Methodist churches. In a fundamental way, the Church of the Nazarene was a product of the Wesleyan holiness movement and one expression of its ideals.

Fundamentalism analyzed the religious problem much differently and generated its own answer. Its foe was "liberalism," a theme underscored by J. Gresham Machen's classic battle text, *Christianity and Liberalism*. The Princeton theologians even regarded holiness theology as a Pelagian highway and thus part of the liberal problem. The evangelists who functioned as the primary spokesmen of the fundamentalist movement were not merely indifferent to the primary concerns of evangelical Wesleyans, but antagonistic to holiness thought. The fundamentalist press generally was unreceptive to holiness thought. To be sure, there are places where the complaints of the Holiness Movement and fundamentalism appeared to intersect. For instance, the prevailing notion in dispensational theology was that the popular churches were apostate and fallen; such a charge could be linked to the holiness complaint that the established churches were formal and cold. The complaints are not actually the same but appear similar, and grassroots Nazarene laity and pastors often responded positively to fundamentalist appeals. Nazarene theologians, however, perceived a danger in the church identifying too closely with the new movement. The primary literature of the fundamentalist cause was written by Calvinists, who wove their basic theology into their attacks on Modernism.

Fundamentalism's intellectual giant was J. Gresham Machen, originally of Princeton and later of Westminster Theological Seminary. Machen and his Presbyterian colleagues skewered Wesleyan-Arminian theology as adeptly as they did Modernist ideas. Nazarene theologians were intent, then, on preventing Reformed theology from taking root in the church through fundamentalism's guise. A. M. Hills' sharp attack on the *Scofield Reference Bible* in the denominational paper is one example of this: "A friend had noted that the Scofield Bible 'has gained a large circulation, and is used extensively by our own people, both by preachers and people.'" Hills lamented this situation, since *Scofield* was "saturated and soaked and dripping with Calvinism and opposition to holiness."[20]

Likewise, H. Orton Wiley published articles in the church paper and in *The Preacher's Magazine* intended to blunt fundamentalism's influence. But his most sustained argument was made when the first volume of *Christian Theology* appeared in 1940. As Paul Bassett convincingly shows, Wiley penned an illuminating passage that discussed "three unworthy Monarchs" that had "scepters falsely thrust into their hands" at different points in Church history. These false authorities include tradition and reason, but he identified the third as the Bible itself. There is a danger, Wiley noted, when appeals to the Bible lapse into a "bibliolatry" that elevates the written word of Scripture to a place of supremacy over the Living Word of Christ. Wiley was writing explicitly about the second period in Protestant theology that followed the Reformation, often dubbed "the Scholastic period," and it was marked by theological rigidity, the drawing of clear lines of demarcation between contending Lutheran and Reformed theologies, and denunciations of those outside the bounds of one's own "orthodoxy." In contrast, Wiley emphasized the subordination of the Written Word to the Personal Word, which is Christ, noting that "the original source of the Christian knowledge of God must ever be, the Lord Jesus Christ." Bassett notes that "Wiley's discerning readers" understood that Protestant Scholasticism's era, and the "false Monarch" of bibliolatry that characterized it, were parallels to the fundamentalist era of Wiley's day.[21]

---

[20] Hills, "The Scofield Reference Bible Examined for the Nazarenes," *Herald of Holiness* (September 10, 1932), p. 3.
[21] Wiley, *Christian Theology*, Vol. 1, pp. 140–43. Paul M. Bassett, "The Fundamentalist Leavening of the Holiness Movement," *Wesleyan Theological Journal* (Spring 1978), pp. 65–67. Wiley's M.A. thesis was a study of the prologue to *John's Gospel*, and "Logos" doctrine remained an important element in his thinking.

H. Orton Wiley and Olive Winchester resisted some of the leading emphases of twentieth-century Fundamentalism.

The spread of dispensational premillenialism was a leading factor in the fundamentalist crusade. The primary Nazarene theologians resisted dispensational theology but approached the issue with different styles and intensity. Teachers of Nazarene theology were honor-bound to stress that the Church of the Nazarene took no stand on behalf of one millennial theory or another. Wiley deflected questions regarding his personal convictions about eschatology, and *Christian Theology* dispassionately surveyed the various viewpoints. Assessments of Wiley's own eschatology differ. Some perceive that Wiley was "most influenced by ... a premillenialism [that is] carefully qualified and nuanced," while others assert that "nearly everybody was wrong, according to Wiley, on eschatology." He was amused by his students' curiosity about his position and by their difficulty in discerning it.[22]

A. M. Hills, on the other hand, deflected nothing. He was an ardent post-millennialist and staunch critic of dispensationalism. That outspokenness played a role when he stepped aside as president of two holiness colleges, and at Pasadena College some students were greatly annoyed that he frequently voiced opposition to premillennialism. At one

---

[22] Harold E. Raser, "Views on Last Things," in H. Ray Dunning, ed., *The Second Coming: A Wesleyan Approach to the Doctrine of Last Things* (Kansas City: Beacon Hill Press of Kansas City, 1995), p. 185. Carl Bangs, *Our Roots of Belief: A Biblical and Faithful Theology* (Kansas City: Beacon Hill Press of Kansas City, 1981), p. 72. Ross Price, "Dr. Wiley—Eminent Theologian," p. 3, a clipping in the H. Orton Wiley profile folder, H. Orton Wiley Collection, Nazarene Archives.

point he was sternly warned by president A.O. Hendricks to tone down his rhetoric or lose his position. When an early draft of his *Fundamental Christian Theology* circulated in the 1910s, he was advised that it would need to say something positive about premillenialism before it could be used as a Nazarene text. When the book appeared some fifteen years later, it included a brief section by J. B. Chapman setting forth the positive argument for premillennialism, thus meeting the earlier objection. Olive Winchester likewise rejected the premillennialism that was spreading within the church. She was an amillennialist and interpreted The Revelation not as predictions of the future but as a coded record of events that had occurred in the biblical writer's own lifetime, most likely during Nero's rule, she thought.[23]

The growth of dispensational premillennialism at the grassroots and its rejection by the church's theological specialists was a small wedge, but over time this difference fostered a growing sense of alienation and suspicion between grassroots Nazarenes and the church's trained theologians. Despite Williams' claim that "every man in this body is a fundamentalist," many features associated with fundamentalism were being resisted in the name of Wesleyan doctrinal clarity. Wiley's emphasis on preserving an Anglo-Methodist view of the "sufficiency of Scripture," Hills' opposition to the *Scofield Reference Bible*, and the resistance of all three of the church's major pre-war theologians to the exclusiveness of dispensational premillenialism contributed to the church's post-war ability to back away from the fundamentalist mentality.

FUNDAMENTALISM LIVES ON

Fundamentalism is hardly dead today. The Evangelical renaissance that followed World War II was designed to move American evangelicals away from fundamentalism's negativity and exclusivity and toward a new critical orthodoxy. Fundamentalists initially decried this move as a betrayal of biblical Christianity, but a subsequent generation has tried to woo evangelicals back into fundamentalist modes of thought. Like their earlier predecessor, today's neo-fundamentalist movements threaten the theological integrity of evangelical denominations by seeking to supplant a Christian organization's founding vision with new ones of the fundamentalists' own devising.

---

[23] Ronald B. Kirkemo, *For Zion's Sake: A History of Pasadena/Point Loma College* (San Diego: Point Loma Press, 1992), p. 93. A. M. Hills, *Fundamental Christian Theology, Abridged Edition*, (Pasadena: C. J. Kinne, 1932), pp. 550–71. Chapman's contribution is on pp. 550–55. Ross Price, "Some Data on Miss Olive Winchester," pp. 7–8, in the Olive Winchester profile folder, Olive Winchester Collection, Nazarene Archives.

One reincarnation of fundamentalism has a political face—the religious-political right. The religious-political right threatens to alter the traditional identities of religious communities by leading them to develop new identities drawn from political culture. In this case, reactionary political beliefs function as hermeneutical lenses, and insights from political life, rather than those drawn from the Bible itself, become "controlling insights" that determine how one reads, understands, and responds to the Christian scriptures. If we apply Fosdick's principle that the difference between conservatives and fundamentalists is the spirit that they bring, then the problem is not that theologically conservative people are also politically conservative; it is the militant conviction that conservative politics are the true legitimate politics of an earnest Christian, and the application of political litmus tests as standards for measuring the spirituality or Christian orthodoxy of another person or religious group. The deep irony is that avatars of the religious-political right threaten the Christian faith with the very thing they so often decry—the danger of reductionism. In their case, they would reduce the faith to a form of mere culture Christianity.

Another way in which Christian fundamentalism is being reincarnated is through new one-issue organizations. These organizations have developed solely to project a single fundamentalist doctrine into as many venues as possible. The Council on Biblical Manhood and Womanhood is a prime example. It exists for the sole purpose of striking one note over and over again. That single note is the assertion of a divinely-sanctioned and scripturally-mandated subordination of women to men in the family and church. The CBMW's officers and advisory board are a "who's who" of Lutheran and Reformed fundamentalist leaders. Its stand on the ordination of women is directly contrary to the historic stand of the Church of the Nazarene and the majority of Wesleyan holiness denominations. The CBMW has its own textbooks: Wayne Grudem and John Piper's *Recovering Biblical Manhood and Womanhood* (1991) and Grudem's *Biblical Foundations for Manhood & Womanhood* (2000). It organizes local chapters in various churches. It has its own website and distributes bundles of pamphlets, booklets, and handouts. CBMW is not concerned with baptismal theology, Christian perfection, or worship wars. It only wants its single message to penetrate as many different congregations and denominations as possible. There are pastors and laity in the Wesleyan tradition who have heard CBMW's siren call and followed it, just as others followed Bill Gothard's teachings on female subordination a generation ago.

The Wesleyan doctrines of grace, faith, and holiness were at the core of the early Nazarene movement, but so, too, was the notion of an "apostolic ministry" in which the gifts and graces, not the gender, of applicants for ordination and ministry were evaluated. The ministry of women was not simply an "add on" to prevailing doctrines of the ministry in late nineteenth- and early twentieth-century Protestantism. Rather, it was a different doctrine of the ministry altogether.[24] CMBW, however, invites Nazarenes to abandon such exegetical, hermeneutical, and theological positions that were central to the vision of the Nazarene founders and substitute its doctrine of the ministry for the Church of the Nazarene's own.

Likewise, the Institute for Creation Research exists to project one fundamentalist idea into as many venues as possible. Its unequivocal emphasis on a literal "six-day creation" is warmly embraced by some religious conservatives as an affirmation of "the old-time religion." Yet Creation science is anything but that. In the late 1970s, Timothy Smith had a standard lecture on the Texas schoolbook controversy of that day. He demonstrated that six-day creationism had long been rejected not only as a mark of evangelical orthodoxy but also as a mark of knowledgeable fundamentalism. As Smith observed, the "day-age" theory and "the gap theory" were two different ways that fundamentalists had reconciled Genesis and modern geology—and done so by abandoning six-day literalism. Ronald Numbers has now documented this in far greater detail, showing the roots of the Institute for Creation Research's thinking in Seventh-Day Adventism, the subsequent appropriation of Adventist thinking by a few committed fundamentalists, and their carefully calibrated campaign to inject those ideas into the mainstream of late-twentieth-century fundamentalism, evangelicalism, and American politics.[25]

While there are numerous instances of Nazarene evangelists and preachers embracing six-day literalism, that viewpoint clearly was not taught as a standard by the denomination in its early years. In 1931, *The Young People's Journal*, a denominational publication for high school youth, published a series on science and religion written by Olive Winchester. In the second essay in the series, Winchester described three scientific theories on the origins of the universe, identifying her own view as the

---

[24] See, for instance, Stan Ingersol, "Your Daughters Shall Prophesy," *Holiness Today* (March 2000): 5–7.
[25] Smith's lecture was one of five delivered at Nazarene Theological Seminary in a January 1979 inter-term course. His lecture on the emerging battle over classroom science texts was titled: "The Old-Time Religion?" Also see Ronald L. Numbers, *The Creationists: The Evolution of Scientific Creationism* (Berkeley: University of California Press, 1992).

"planetismal theory." It held that the observable universe developed as gravitational forces caused matter to coalesce over long eons of time. A. M. Hills embraced the identical view when he discussed the Christian doctrine of creation in his two volume *Fundamental Christian Theology*. While neither affirmed biological evolution, Winchester and Hills embraced cosmic and geological evolution without compunction. H. Orton Wiley likewise believed in an ancient earth and saw numerous parallels between the Genesis account of creation and the discoveries of modern science. The Institute for Creation Research and its acolytes suggest that anything less than six-day literalism is compromise with the spirit of the age, yet these examples from early Nazarene history demonstrate otherwise.[26]

As the Institute for Creation Research's influence is exerted in evangelical denominations, evangelicals would be wise to question what, exactly, ICR asks of them. It asks evangelicals to reject notions of an ancient cosmos and an ancient earth and retreat from the perspectives that dominated the Evangelical renaissance of the post-World War II era, when Carl F. H. Henry, Bernard Ramm, Timothy Smith, and a generation of respected evangelical leaders tried to move religious conservatives away from fundamentalism. These leaders regarded fundamentalism as contracted, pessimistic, and completely inadequate for meeting the challenges Protestantism would face in the modern world. Their very complaint was that early twentieth-century fundamentalism had distorted orthodox Protestantism. The Institute for Creation Research, however, regards the giants of post-war evangelicalism as misguided and bids evangelicals to follow its lesser light. Even more, it bids Nazarenes to reject the perspectives of their own denomination's first generation theologians and accept an obscurantism that is neither native to it nor wise.

The Church of the Nazarene's encounter with fundamentalism has been a long one, for the denomination was formed in the same century in which fundamentalism took shape as a movement. Nazarenes and fundamentalism have grown up together. At times Nazarenes have even chosen to be bedfellows with fundamentalism. But the Nazarenes were the product of a different movement with a very different core of theological ideas; their spiritual life is the expression of a different essential quality. If they are wise, these are truths they will never forget.

---

[26] *Young People's Journal* (January 1931): 3–4, (May 1931): 3–4, (June 1931): 4, and other issues in passim. A. M. Hills, *Fundamental Christian Theology*, Vol. 1, pp. 263–79. H. Orton Wiley, *Christian Theology*, Vol. 1, pp. 454–458, 462–66.

Chapter 5
Nazarene Odyssey and the Hinges of Internationalization

When the 25th General Assembly of the Church of the Nazarene convened in June 2001, 40 percent of the 995 registered voting delegates either spoke English as a second language or not at all. Some of the delegates elected by districts in developing nations were unable to attend the assembly, so this percentage would have surpassed 45 percent in a more perfect world.[1]

The Church of the Nazarene originated as a denominational expression of the North American holiness movement, but by 2013 the Nazarenes had an official presence in 159 world areas and were an international denomination of 455 districts, of which only eighty were in the United States and Canada.[2] Over half of the denomination's members have been citizens of nations other than the U.S. and Canada since 1998, and Canadian and American representatives became a minority on the church's General Board in 2001. By 2013, the American and Canadian "share" was 30 percent of the church's total members, while 28 percent were in Latin American and the Caribbean, and 26 percent were in Africa. Moreover, if present demographic trends continue, the percentage of Nazarenes who reside in Asia, Africa, the Pacific, the Caribbean, and Latin America will increase steadily. The number of Nazarenes in nations of the old Soviet bloc, where the church has established footholds, will also increase, bringing further diversity to the denomination.

These trends have had a definite impact on the church's General Assembly, where binding decisions upon the denomination are made. Liberation theologians speak rightly of the need for a self-critical principle to be engaged in the work of theological reflection. Ironically, the Nazarenes, regarded as theologically conservative, have brought a self-critical principle into their highest governing body through the international structure of their church and the global diversity of their General Assembly. American

---
[1]   From statistical information provided to the writer by Shirley Marvin, Office of the General Secretary, Church of the Nazarene.
[2]   Office of the General Secretary, Church of the Nazarene, "The Church at Work: General Statistics by Region, 2012 Statistical Year."

mainline denominations struggle to ensure that many different voices are heard at their general meetings and often establish racial quotas to ensure this. Nazarenes, who have never adopted quotas, hold a quadrennial general meeting that may be the most racially diverse general meeting of any denomination that originated in North America. There, American assumptions regarding doctrine and governance are challenged by delegates with Asian, African, or Latin American perspectives—among others.

The Church of the Nazarene's evolution from an American church into an international one invites attention. The autonomous national church was long a staple of Protestantism, adopted first by Lutheran and Reformed churches, and later by Anglicans and Methodists. Believers' churches, such as Mennonites, Baptists, and Quakers, likewise follow this pattern. Protestants were not the first, of course. Eastern Orthodoxy has also been organized around denominations that represent spheres of national and cultural influence. But delegates to the Twentieth General Assembly of the Church of the Nazarene [1980] rejected this path of development and embraced *internationalization*, a philosophy that envisioned the church as a global *ecclesia* of districts and congregations rather than a fellowship of autonomous national churches.[3]

What are the hinges on which this story turns? This chapter examines two. *How* did a "mission to the world" become a Nazarene priority? And *why* was it possible for those who recommended internationalization in 1980, and the General Assembly that embraced it, to think outside the usual Protestant box?

A Mission to the World

A strong sense of "mission to the world" emerged early in Nazarene life, and this impulse should be viewed within the wider history of Protestant missions. Like the American holiness movement that spawned it, the Church of the Nazarene is a denomination rooted in the ethos of Protestant Pietism, a way of being Protestant that has a distinct and deep

---

[3] See the report of the first Commission on Internationalization, *Journal of the Twentieth General Assembly of the Church of the Nazarene* (Kansas City: Nazarene Publishing House, 1980), pp. 232–38. This first commission, authorized in 1976 by the Nineteenth General Assembly, was re-authorized by each subsequent General Assembly until the Twenty-Fourth General Assembly in 1997, when no commissions were authorized. This series of study commissions continued to evaluate and refine the principles and practice of internationalization, reporting to the General Board and to the General Assembly. Also see Jerald D. Johnson, *The International Experience* (Kansas City: Nazarene Publishing House, 1982); and Franklin Cook, *The International Dimension* (Kansas City: Nazarene Publishing House, 1984), esp. pp. 48–64.

tradition of missions. One particular strain of Pietist missionary influence runs from the University of Halle into the Moravians, influences British and American Methodism, and is reflected in the witness of the various Wesleyan holiness churches. It is as if a code is genetically imprinted on churches that stand in dynamic relationship to historic Methodism. Beyond that, there are wider currents in British and American religion, such as the rise of dispensational premillennialism, that also foster the missionary impulse.

But the high priority that Nazarenes gave to a "mission to the world" by 1925 was facilitated also by institutional needs connected intimately to the denomination's birth. The Pentecostal Church of the Nazarene (as it was known until 1919) was produced by a series of mergers between much smaller churches that were regional in nature. The first key merger occurred in 1907, when the Church of the Nazarene, whose churches were located predominantly along the West Coast, merged with the Association of Pentecostal Churches of America, a predominantly East Coast body. In 1908 the Holiness Church of Christ, based in the South, merged with them. On a gamut of theological issues, the merging churches shared a common set of basic convictions, but they differed in governance, leadership style, priorities, and emphasis.[4] Each brought a publishing house to the united church, and three separate church papers continued to be published through 1911, a situation that reinforced regionalism at the risk of undermining unity. Early leaders, particularly general superintendents P. F. Bresee and H. F. Reynolds, sought to rally the uniting bodies to a set of common priorities, seeking to integrate them and achieve what Timothy Smith later called "the inner reality of union." As the new denomination began to subordinate regional priorities and establish common ones, the commitment to a "mission to the world" advanced steadily to the top.

The Critical Advocacy of H. F. Reynolds

Hiram F. Reynolds' leadership was closely connected to this development. Reynolds served as one of the church's general superintendents from 1907 to 1932, becoming the senior general superintendent upon Bresee's death in 1915. Reynolds was then 61, and his influence on Nazarene life, already considerable, emerged more forcefully.

Reynolds was born and raised near Chicago. His father's early death led to the breakup of his family. By seven he had moved in with neighboring

---

[4] The alignment of the merging churches on a variety of theological issues is analyzed in "Methodism and the Theological Identity of the Church of the Nazarene," *Methodist History* (Oct. 2004): 17–32.

farmers who had no child of their own. His upbringing was largely devoid of religious influences. The first person to speak meaningfully about religion to him was a sister-in-law, a Methodist, with whom he became better acquainted after moving into Chicago in his late teens. But he never came under the church's influence until his early 20s, when he went to Vermont to visit his mother, who had relocated there many years before. Reynolds was converted in New England through Methodist influences, studied for the ministry at a Methodist seminary, and was ordained by Bishop John Hurst. He entered the ministry of the Vermont Conference in 1879, serving several charges before entering fulltime work as a revivalist. In 1895 he transferred his credentials to the Association of Pentecostal Churches of America and moved to Brooklyn, New York. At the First General Assembly of the Pentecostal Church of the Nazarene in 1907, the uniting bodies elected Bresee and Reynolds as the first two general superintendents of the new church.[5] Reynolds shared Bresee's Methodist background and the latter's belief in the necessity of a general superintendency. He also shared Bresee's understanding that general superintendency had to be limited in scope within a democratic system of church governance. As an evangelist, he had learned to rely on powers of persuasion. Like Bresee, he wore superintendency well and endeavored to model a leadership style that inspired the confidence of others.

Despite their similarities, Bresee and Reynolds had two different visions of what the Church of the Nazarene should be. Their visions meshed at certain points; both visions stressed the importance of evangelism, for instance. But their visions were not identical.

Bresee believed that the Church of the Nazarene's primary purpose was to "Christianize Christianity," a term he employed frequently. He believed that the integrity of the Gospel was at stake in American culture and in wider Christendom. He shared H. C. Morrison's assessment that "there is a stiffness and coldness in [Methodism's] city churches that freeze out the common people, and, worst of all shuts out the Christ of the common people. The pastors of our city churches are not soul winners."[6] Bresee's answer was direct: bypass establishment Methodism and take

---

[5] The basic details of Reynolds' life are found in Amy N. Hinshaw's *In Labors Abundant: A Biography of H. F. Reynolds, D.D.* (Kansas City: Nazarene Publishing House, n.d. [ca. 1939]). Reynolds has not yet been the subject of a critical biography, though his influence on the Church of the Nazarene and in the history of Protestant missions certainly merits the attention.

[6] *Pentecostal Herald* (January 25, 1899). Quoted by Charles Edwin Jones in "The Holiness Complaint with Late-Victorian Methodism" in Russell E. Richey and Kenneth E. Rowe, eds., *Rethinking Methodist History: A Bicentennial Historical Consultation* (Nashville: Kingswood Books, 1985), p. 59.

the Gospel back to the urban poor. Bresee's vision for the Church of the Nazarene centered almost entirely around "building up centers of holy fire" in America's great urban centers. He was not opposed to cross-cultural missions at all, but they were not his passion. At the time of the first merger in 1907, the Nazarenes on the West Coast, after over twelve years of Bresee's leadership, had taken no initiative to open a single field overseas. Their only mission work outside North America—the Hope School for Girls in Calcutta, India—was founded by two residents of India—an English woman and an Indian woman—who had sought an American sponsor and found it in Bresee.

Reynolds brought a very different vision to the Pentecostal Church of the Nazarene. His was a vision of world evangelization. In 1897, the Association of Pentecostal Churches of America elected him to be their secretary of home and foreign missions, and the first group of five missionaries was sent to India later that year. Reynolds served continuously as the secretary of home and foreign missions until the merger of regional churches. He began conducting revivals in Canada in 1898 and organized two congregations in Nova Scotia in 1902. The missions in India were steadily reinforced with new personnel and the number of stations expanded. And in 1901, John Diaz, a Cape Verdean immigrant, was sent back to his native islands to open missions and churches there. Under Reynolds' leadership, the Association of Pentecostal Churches of America sent out 18 missionaries between 1897and 1907.

In his dual role as general superintendent and general missionary secretary, Hiram F. Reynolds articulated a vision of world evangelization that captured the imagination of Nazarenes and laid the foundations of the church's international character.

Thirteen were in active service in 1905, supported by fewer than 50 congregations in the United States and Canada. Reynolds brought to the united church his experience as a missions executive who could articulate a positive basis for worldwide missions and organize and motivate people for carrying out that purpose, including the raising of necessary funds.7

---

7 A useful table listing all missionaries connected with the Church of the Nazarene through 1930 and their fields of service can be found in *The Other Sheep* (November 1930): 30–31.

Others in the church shared Reynolds' vision of worldwide missions at the time of the 1907/1908 mergers. Leslie Gay, a layman, and Maye McReynolds, a clergywoman, were close associates of Bresee who shared this passion for missions. By 1920, other Bresee associates—including C. J. Kinne and Ada Glidden Bresee—emerged as leading figures in the missions movement within the Church of the Nazarene.8 In the South, the Holiness Church of Christ had missionaries in India and Mexico at the time of the mergers and was in the process of sending missionaries to Japan. These various forces were consolidated under Reynolds' leadership after the Second General Assembly in 1908.

Reynolds' primary role in shaping Nazarene life from 1907 on sprang from dual roles that he held simultaneously for many years: those of general superintendent *and* general missionary secretary. He was an active general superintendent until 1932. He was also executive secretary of foreign missions from 1907–22 and 1925–27. Before the First General Assembly in 1907, Reynolds was limited to promoting his vision of worldwide missions among churches of the eastern seaboard. His canvas expanded greatly after the merger, which gave him contact with congregations in the West, Midwest, and South. More importantly, the united church had a system of governance different from what the eastern congregations had known before the merger. In the new order, Reynolds was responsible, as a general superintendent, to conduct district assemblies. And in his capacity as general missionary secretary, he was now positioned to communicate his passion for cross-cultural missions at every district assembly that he conducted. From 1907 on, he urged Pentecostal Nazarenes at ever-larger district and general gatherings to rally to this cause.

Reynolds embarked on the first world tour of Nazarene missions in December 1913. The journey proved a vital step, reaping public relations benefits and establishing an important principle regarding the general superintendency. Reynolds left San Francisco accompanied by ten Nazarene missionaries headed for their assignments in Japan, China, and India. He spent nearly one month in Japan, visiting the mission work in Kyoto, contacting the mission superintendents of other denominations and groups, and surveying Japanese cities where no Nazarene work yet existed. The latter was important; he wanted to be better informed when

---

[8] Kinne was the founding manager of the Nazarene Publishing House in Kansas City. After returning to California, he lectured on missions in Nazarene churches on the West Coast. He conceived of a hospital in Japan, organized the funds to build it, and managed the construction of Bresee Memorial Hospital in Tamingfu, China. His first wife died during the project, and Kinne subsequently married Sue Bresee, Phineas Bresee's daughter. Ada Glidden Bresee was Phineas Bresee's daughter-in-law.

corresponding in the future with missionaries and national leaders in Japan. He spent the next month in China following a similar pattern.

His visit to India turned into something different and grittier. In Calcutta he discovered that a situation existed that required him to carefully consider the careers of a missionary couple and the native superintendent of the Hope School for Girls. This unexpected turn of affairs forced Reynolds to discard his itinerary and remain in India for nearly three months, much of it confined to Calcutta, where eventually he dismissed missionaries and national workers, received resignations from others, and reorganized the staff of the mission. He remained until L. S. Tracy could transfer from Western India some weeks later. The Calcutta experience was a critical moment for Reynolds, who was committed to careful missions policy ever afterward.

He resumed the world tour that summer, reaching Swaziland in the second week of July, where he examined the work led by Harmon Schmelzenbach. He then passed through the Cape Verde Islands. Naval hostilities between England and Germany prevented Reynolds from making his scheduled visit to the Nazarene work in Cape Verde, but he did contact civil officials. He reached Scotland, where he visited George Sharpe and the congregations of the Pentecostal Church of Scotland, encouraging the merger of that denomination with the Pentecostal Nazarenes in the following year. Reynolds finally arrived in New York City over eight months after starting his journey.[9]

The worldwide mission tour was valuable on several levels. It added depth to Reynolds' own perceptions of missionary life. Amy Hinshaw, his biographer, summarized the salient points:

> As a rule, officials holding high positions visit their church enterprises after they have become valuable assets to the denomination. But Dr. Reynolds toured the missions of the Church of the Nazarene in the pioneer days when they were weak and small ... Hotels and comfortable homes were not available. So [he viewed] pioneer missionary life at close range, with its sterner features in the foreground and conspicuously outlined. ... [H]e adapted himself to

---

[9] The details are found in H. F. Reynolds, *World-Wide Missions* (Kansas City: Publishing House of the Pentecostal Church of the Nazarene, 1915), except for those concerning the firing of missionaries and workers in Calcutta. Those are documented in J. Timothy White's "Hiram F. Reynolds: Prime Mover of the Nazarene Mission Education System" (University of Kansas, PhD. Dissertation, 1996). White's account of Reynolds's reorganization of the Calcutta mission, and its impact on his thinking, is told on pp. 113–54.

the conditions that prevailed. He slept on the dirt floors in Chinese inns, and rode in "rickshaws" and springless carts, and second rate trains, in gharries and tongas and covered wagons; he waded through snow-drifts in China, and traveled under the tropical sun in India in the hottest season of the year, and he penetrated even the malaria-infested "bushveldts" in Africa.[10]

The worldwide mission tour proved invaluable for promoting missions. Reynolds took one of the new Brownie cameras with him and generated hundreds of photographs, some of which were published in the church's monthly missions magazine, *The Other Sheep*.[11] Likewise he generated a steady stream of travel commentary for the weekly church paper. And soon after his return to America he published *World-Wide Missions* (1915), a book illustrated with his photographs.

The tour also established the principle that the role of the general superintendent in the Church of the Nazarene was to be *general* in a manner broad enough that it engaged the missions and churches outside the United States and Canada. Reynolds became convinced that the church's highest officials should not rely simply on reports from the field. He became a staunch advocate of regular visitation of the churches and missions in other nations by the members of the Board of General Superintendents, and he set the example repeatedly. In 1916 he visited Cuba and Central America. In 1919 he returned to Japan and China. In 1921 he returned to the British Isles, South Africa, and India, and visited the Middle East, where there were now churches and missions in Syria and Palestine.

Reynolds made his third trip to Japan and China in 1922, presiding at the Japan District's first district assembly, at which pastor J. I. Nagamatsu was elected district superintendent. In 1927 he visited the Caribbean and organized the Trinidad and Barbados Districts. In 1927 he planned a second worldwide tour since none of his colleagues seemed inclined to duplicate his original worldwide tour. His brethren on the Board of General Superintendents were convinced it would kill the 74-year-old man. Reynolds relented only when the 1928 General Assembly determined that general superintendents John Goodwin and R. T. Williams would

---

[10] Hinshaw, *In Labors Abundant*, pp. 259–60.
[11] The H. F. Reynolds Collection in the Nazarene Archives contains over 2000 photographs, many of which Reynolds received from others, but many photographs taken by him. Nearly 1000 of his negatives are preserved. The quality of the photos he took varies widely.

conduct a worldwide tour together, which they did in 1929–30. Neither enjoyed the experience, and Williams intentionally avoided overseas travel after that. But Reynolds had made his point: if general superintendency was not local or regional in character, neither could it be allowed to simply be national in scope by default; to be true *general superintendency*, it had to be international in character.[12]

That point was not lost on Goodwin, who carried out his share of international visitations, nor on J. B. Chapman, who was elected a general superintendent in 1928 and began making international trips three years later.[13]

During the years that Reynolds was executive secretary of the General Board of Foreign Missions, it became the most impressive denominational agency established by action of the General Assembly, attracting the lion's share of monies given voluntarily to general interests. Reynolds' ability to communicate his missionary vision and inspire others to share it is ample testimony to his dogged determination and persuasive powers during the years of his greatest effectiveness. Cross-cultural missions became the denomination's most important priority and functioned as an integrating concept within the church. Bresee fashioned the church's basic mechanisms of governance, but Reynolds laid the foundations of a missions program that resulted in the Church of the Nazarene entering the twenty-first century as a global denomination. When Reynolds died in 1938, Chapman's funeral oration hailed him appropriately as "the original missionary" of the Nazarene movement.[14]

WOMEN'S VOLUNTARY SOCIETIES

The creation of two general auxiliaries, one for youth and one for women, also played key roles in unifying the church. Each strengthened the sinews binding the Pentecostal Nazarenes into one people. But the network of lay and clergy women who formed the Woman's Missionary Society also

---

[12] J. B. Chapman, *A History of the Church of the Nazarene* (Kansas City: Nazarene Publishing House, 1926), pp. 142–43. In a classic understatement, Chapman noted that "it would be difficult to give any adequate account of the many and varied activities of Dr. Reynolds since he entered the General Superintendency." The Reynolds Collection in the Nazarene Archives bears out that truth. It contains over 25,000 pieces of correspondence, very little of it addressed to Reynolds' home or office. His correspondents had to follow his published itinerary in the church paper and send mail to him in transit. He traveled with a portable typewriter and banged out replies.

[13] J. B. Chapman's *30,000 Miles of Missionary Travel* (Kansas City: Nazarene Publishing House, n.d. [ca. 1931]) recounts his trip to Central and South America, the British West Indies, Africa, and Great Britain.

[14] J. B. Chapman, "Excerpts From the Memorial Sermon for Dr. Reynolds." Typescript. J. B. Chapman Collection, Nazarene Archives, Lenexa, Kansas.

came to play an important role in promoting missions and raising it to a denominational priority. By 1930 a majority of Nazarene congregations had local mission society chapters, and they existed not only in the West but in Asia, Africa, Latin America, and the Middle East.

The rise of the Woman's Missionary Society is a theme in two different chapters of Nazarene history: missions history and the story of women and religion. Only single women had "careers" in late nineteenth- and early twentieth-century America; married women did not. But a growing number of married women who were part of the growing middle class gained a degree of leisure time due to the increased availability of canned foods and manufactured clothing, and the spread of labor-saving devices. They filled this time by forming voluntary societies. Some societies were literary and cultural in nature. But as social historian Anne Firor Scott noted, many women were convinced "that if their families needed them less, the Lord had work for them to do," and they created voluntary societies with religious purposes. John P. McDowell has demonstrated how the women's home mission movement in the Methodist Episcopal Church, South, not only raised money for home evangelism but became a leading agent of socially-minded Christianity, spearheading an anti-lynching campaign and working for social improvements for Southern blacks.[15] Women's voluntary societies expanded in nearly all Protestant denominations. In the case of the Nazarenes, however, the rise of the Woman's Missionary Society was different from its analogues in other denominations, for it was distinctly a partnership between lay women and clergy women. This is exemplified in the leadership roles assumed from 1915 on by Rev. Susan Fitkin of Brooklyn, New York, a former evangelist, and Ada Glidden Bresee, a lay woman active in the affairs of the Southern California District.

The Eastern parent body, where Reynolds headed the missions program, took the lead in developing the Woman's Missionary Society. Stella Reynolds, his wife, and Susan Fitkin, a former Quaker evangelist, organized a series of congregation-based societies beginning in 1898. The rudiments of a general system of societies were in place by the time of the 1907 merger but were scrapped during the merger itself. Still, local societies remained a part of congregational life in the East, and some society members persistently advocated that other churches organize societies and

---

[15] Anne Firor Scott, "The 'New Woman' in the New South," in *Making the Invisible Woman Visible* (Urbana and Chicago: University of Illinois Press, 1984), p. 198. And John Patrick McDowell, *The Social Gospel in the South: The Woman's Home Mission Movement in the Methodist Episcopal Church, South, 1886–1939* (Baton Rouge: Louisiana State University Press, 1982).

even argued for district and general organizations as well. The Fourth General Assembly (1915) authorized the leaders of the movement to create a constitution for a general WMS, and the Fifth General Assembly (1919) approved the plan. Fitkin served as general WMS president from 1915 to 1948. The stated purposes were to promote the missions within the church through advocacy, education, and fundraising. Until 1932, the funds raised by the mission society chapters were channeled directly into missions and nothing else.[16]

The spread of local chapters in the early 1920s met resistance from some clergy, who viewed the local society chapter and its female leaders as threats to their own leadership within the congregation. This attitude slowly changed over time. For one thing, the chapters proved helpful to the church program. But pastors soon recognized another undeniable fact: the sharply increasing number of women who joined and participated in the society chapters. The growth of the WMS was evidence of two things: women sought affinity with one another, and the missions movement in the Church of the Nazarene was growing in strength with each passing year. In 1920 only a little more than eight percent of Nazarenes belonged to the Woman's Missionary Society. By 1930, the first year that a majority of Nazarene congregations had a local chapter, that percentage had risen to nearly twenty-seven percent. By 1935, eight-five percent of congregations had a society chapter and thirty-two percent of all Nazarenes belonged to one.[17]

MISSIONS AND THE MILLENNIUM

The reprioritizing of Nazarene life around cross-cultural missions was assisted by premillenialism's growth within the denomination. The roots of the Protestant missionary enterprise of the nineteenth century largely lay in postmillennialism, not premillennialism. But the premillennial movement that spread through American churches after 1875 brought added passion for missions.[18] There is no better evidence than the rise of the Pentecostals, whose intense premillennial anticipations stirred equally strong missionary enthusiasms.

---

[16] Fitkin's autobiography is *Grace Much More Abounding* (Kansas City: Nazarene Publishing House, n.d.). Also see Basil Miller's *Susan N. Fitkin: For God and Missions* (Kansas City: Nazarene Publishing House, n. d. [ca. 1948]).
[17] These percentages were calculated from statistical tables IX and X in the *General Secretary's Report to the Twenty-third General Assembly*. See Journal of the Twenty-third General Assembly (Kansas City: Nazarene Publishing House, 1993), pp. 274–79.
[18] See Timothy P. Weber, *Living in the Shadow of the Second Coming: American Premillenialism, 1875–1982* (Grand Rapids, Mich.: Acadamie Books [Zondervan]: 1983), pp. 65–81.

Harold Raser has written a useful survey of millennial perspectives within the larger American holiness movement, but no detailed study has been published on the growth of premillennialism among Nazarenes.[19] The denomination officially supported no particular millennial theory, but articles and letters in the *Herald of Holiness* give ample evidence that premillenialism, with an ever larger share of adherents, was becoming the dominant eschatological perspective of evangelists, pastors, and lay people. B. F. Haynes, C. W. Ruth, J. B. Chapman, and E. P. Ellyson were among the early leaders who shared this view. In 1915, the church absorbed J. O. McClurkan's Pentecostal Mission, bringing in a mission-minded group of churches and workers in the southeastern United States and new mission fields in Cuba, Guatemala, and India. Many of McClurkan's followers shared his earnest conviction that this was "the eleventh hour" before Christ's return; therefore missions was the urgent issue of the day. As premillennialism gained adherents within the Church of the Nazarene, it intensified the priority given to cross-cultural missions.[20]

CONSEQUENCES OF THE PRIORITY OF MISSIONS

The reprioritizing of Nazarene life around world evangelization soon touched every aspect of the church's life. It spurred the development of the church's General Board and general budget in 1923, and it transformed the primary means through which Nazarenes carried out social ministry.

Nazarenes had embraced social work as integral to ministry in Christ's name from their earliest years. Their original patterns of social ministry centered on the maintenance and support of orphanages and homes for unwed mothers. But as missions emerged as a dominant priority for the denomination, the compassionate impulse was rechanneled overseas, where it centered ever more on medical ministries. From the 1920s through the '60s, Nazarenes built, on average, one new hospital a decade, beginning in the 1920s with hospitals in Swaziland and China, then in India and later Papua New Guinea. The Samaritan Hospital, established in Nampa, Idaho, served the overseas medical network by training nurses to serve in mission settings. Each hospital overseas was both a surgical facility and the

---

[19] Harold Raser, "Views on Last Things in the American Holiness Movement," in H. Ray Dunning, ed., *The Second Coming: A Wesleyan Approach to the Doctrine of Last Things* (Kansas City: Beacon Hill Press of Kansas City, 1995), pp. 161–85.

[20] J. O. McClurkan, "The Eleventh Hour Laborers," *Chosen Vessels* (Salem, Ohio: Allegheny Wesleyan Methodist Connection, 1978 [reprint]), pp. 191–99; Mildred Wynkoop, *The Trevecca Story* (Nashville: Trevecca Press, 1976), pp. 32–38; and William J. Strickland and H. Ray Dunning, *J. O. McClurkan: His Life, His Theology, and Selections from His Writings* (Nashville: Trevecca Press, 1998), pp. 91–93.

hub of a more extended network of clinics and mobile "field work" teams who reached out into areas that were remote.[21]

The gradual institutionalization of the compassionate impulse around medical ministries overseas and away from orphanages or homes for unwed mothers at home reflected a fundamental fact: the growing mania for cross-cultural missions was changing denominational priorities and reshaping the inner life of the Church of the Nazarene. By 1950 the Church of the Nazarene's rules, seasonal revivals, and passion for missions were the three elements that defined much of what it was and did.

Internationalization's Hinge

The Church of the Nazarene's growth around the world was slow but not always steady until after World War II. Serious financial setbacks that began in the mid-1920s diminished the church's ability to put wings under its dreams. In the late '20s, the policy of "retrenchment" resulted in mission stations closing and furloughed missionaries forced out of service because the church could not continue supporting them in the field. The situation improved some in the 1930s, but significant change waited until a rising tide of prosperity began during World War II. The church treasury benefited greatly from this, and the stage was set for rapid missionary expansion in the post-war era.

Indigenous holiness churches in Australia and Italy united with the Nazarenes in the late 1940s, providing their first foothold on the only inhabited continents where they had lacked a presence. The church began mission work in the Philippines, a key field, and reorganized work in Korea and Japan that had been undermined by the war. A new field was entered almost every other year. In the 1950s and 1960s, two conservative groups in the United States broke off from the Church of the Nazarene and started new denominations, convinced that Nazarenes had abandoned first principles and lost their fervor along with their way. Yet, the greatest period of mission expansion in Nazarene history came after these groups left, not before that. In the last quarter of the twentieth century, the number of world areas in which the church ministered doubled, and the number of Nazarenes nearly tripled. The bulk of that growth was the direct outgrowth of missions and internationalization, and that pace of growth continues today.

The forms of ministry also changed. The traditional global ministries—evangelism, education, and medicine—were joined by new ministries of

---

[21] For more details and analysis, see Chapter 3 on the stages of Nazarene social ministry.

famine and disaster relief, child sponsorship, and economic development coordinated through Nazarene Compassionate Ministries. Thousands of ordinary American, Canadian, and British Nazarenes went to the very mission fields they had long supported to engage in construction projects by joining Work and Witness Teams. And Nazarenes in Voluntary Service has placed hundreds of others overseas in short-term mission assignments of two years or so. Perhaps nothing illustrates the international character of the church better than this fact: a growing number of missionaries appointed by the General Board of the Church of the Nazarene are citizens of non-Western nations.[22]

The Global Nazarene Theology Conference held in April 2002 in Guatemala City was another major symbol of internationalization in Nazarene life. Earlier Nazarene theology conferences had included representatives from outside North America, but the 2002 conference was far different: it brought together three hundred theological educators, pastors, and church administrators at a location outside American soil. Half of those in attendance were neither American nor Canadian, and academic papers and leadership assignments were distributed in ways that elicited the broadest possible participation. This was followed in 2007 by a second international theology conference held in The Netherlands, with similar conferences scheduled for the future.[23]

The path to internationalization is a main theme in Nazarene history. But why was it possible for Nazarenes to remain one international body instead of breaking into autonomous national churches? Why did the course of Nazarene history run into a channel so different from that of older Protestant denominations?

The answer turns very simply on this: the distinction between hierarchically structured churches and democratically structured ones. The Roman Catholic Church, the Church of Jesus Christ of Latter Day Saints, and The Church of Christ, Scientist, chose to be international churches and had the ability to do so at early points in their history because they are hierarchically structured.

But democratically structured churches had no such option until recently, for democratic governance requires church representatives

---

[22] The most recent history of Nazarene missions that touches most of these points, is J. Fred Parker's *Mission to the World: A History of Missions in the Church of the Nazarene Through 1985* (Kansas City: Nazarene Publishing House, 1988).

[23] All papers of the Global Nazarene Theology Conference are posted at the following Web site: http://wesley.nnu.edu/2002-GNTC/. The papers from Global Theology Conference II are available online in English and Spanish at: http://didache.nazarene.org/index.php?option=com_content&do_pdf=1&id=19.

to assemble regularly for legislative deliberation and action. Nearly all Protestant churches have embodied some type of democratic governance. Until the twentieth century, the modes of transportation have made it difficult, if not impossible, for a church to be both democratic in spirit and international in scope.

Timing, they say, is everything. The Church of the Nazarene originated as a democratic form of Methodism and would have shared the same constraints of older Protestant churches except that it originated in the twentieth century and benefited from that century's technological advances. The transportation and communications revolutions of the twentieth century had altered mental horizons and changed the basic calculus of the situation by the time Nazarenes needed to confront the issues involving its churches throughout the world. When the 1976 General Assembly appointed a commission to study the denomination's future development, modern communications had made it possible for church leaders on opposite sides of the world to maintain routine contact. The development of the modern airline industry quickly after World War II made it possible to regularly assemble delegates from around the world for General Assembly, General Board, and even routine committee assignments. When Nazarenes pondered the denomination's future shape in the 1970s, the most significant factor that facilitated internationalization was not an ideal embedded within the report of the Commission on the International Church but something wholly outside it—technological change. The technological revolutions of the twentieth century allowed the Church of the Nazarene to choose a brand new path while retaining its basic character as a form of democratic Methodism. Modern technology was the primary hinge upon which the internationalization of the Church of the Nazarene swung.

This raises a final question: if new methods of transportation and communications are what changed the Nazarenes, then are they truly unique in their development into an international denomination with a democratic constitution, or are they merely riding the crest of the wave of the future?

There is evidence that the latter is the case. The United Methodist Church embraced a new pattern of denominational development in its 1996 General Conference. The new approach is called "globalization" (an unfortunate term with connotations too closely related to notions of the West's economic hegemony). The assumptions that United Methodists adopted resemble closely those that Nazarenes embraced in 1980. United Methodist "central conferences" located outside the United States may still choose national autonomy, but this course is no longer inevitable as a matter of policy or necessity. If African and Asian conferences remain within the United Methodist Church, this will have a major impact on United Methodism's future, since church members in the developing world tend to be evangelicals with a vibrant faith and traditional views of sexual morality. Moreover, four of the five United Methodist jurisdictions in the U.S. have a negative growth rate (the more traditionalist Southeastern Jurisdiction is the exception), while United Methodists in Africa, Asia, and Russia are producing a positive growth rate. Still, with 7.9 million United Methodists in the U.S. and only 3.5 million outside, it may be several more decades before Americans become a minority within the United Methodist denomination. But United Methodism's turn toward "globalization" suggests that the social and technological revolutions of the twentieth century are influencing one of America's major Protestant denominations and changing the way it positions itself in the world. Will other denominations follow suit? And what, especially, about the young denominations that have originated in the past half-century? Will their missionary enthusiasms eventually result in any of them becoming international denominations, or will their particular forms of governance (often congregational in form) prohibit such a development?

The first century of the Nazarene experience is now clear. Emerging as an early twentieth century denomination from the landscape of scattered holiness denominations, the Nazarenes, like the Wesleyan Church, became a major ingathering church of the Wesleyan holiness revival. Early in their history, Nazarenes committed their resources to world evangelization and evolved in less than a century into an international denomination of many peoples and languages. At the beginning, they came from many groups to become one. When they went out into the world, they again became many, but within the compass of a single international church.

Chapter 6
Past and Prospect

In *Requiem for a Nun,* one of William Faulkner's characters famously says: "The past is never dead. It's not even past." Faulkner was a product of the American South, which historian Carl Degler described as a region that emphasizes "place over time," and where time, accordingly, always seems to linger in the background while class and status stand squarely in front. But even when time recedes from our consciousness, its influence never disappears. The past continually exerts a subtle influence, or as novelist Sarah Dessen puts it, "even if you forget it, it remembers you."[1]

Yet, the past has vanished from the imaginations of some people. They disregard history because they view it as nostalgic and sentimental, and they are neither. Or they had a bad experience with antiquarianism, in which someone created a fetish from some relic of the past. Or they consider themselves "forward-looking people" and ignore history because giving it attention violates their self-image. For whatever reason, they view the past as a distraction, or worse, an impediment. The idea that their past and future are bound together is alien to them.

But the future is never unbounded or totally free. History, which sets today's table, has been setting tomorrow's as well. So one of the surest grounds upon which to engage the future is to know how things stand presently, how present circumstances were assembled, and how the present and future grow out of the past. Historical inquiry is neither nostalgic nor antiquarian; it is a process that acquires useful knowledge of the forces that shaped our lives and are shaping our future. It reflects on these forces. It seeks to understand how we have constructed personal and social identities through our participation in the world and in society.

For Christians, church history is also about something more: it is about understanding how our lives are shaped by a Christian faith that is

---

[1] William Faulkner, *Requiem for a Nun* (New York: Vintage, 2011): 73. Sarah Dessen, *What Happened to Goodbye* (New York: Viking, 2011): 285.

deeply historical, and how we have been incorporated into the Church's wider story.

In the aftermath of the Church of the Nazarene's centennial year, as we look both to the past and to the future—our *heritage* and our *hope*—it is worth remembering that the issues Nazarenes will encounter have grown out of our past. The way in which the past intrudes on the present makes it worthy of our attention. From this perspective, we examine four issues in which the past is shaping our future.

Do Nazarenes Still Have a Knack for Organization?

Early Nazarenes were remarkably adept at attracting families and entire congregations from other Wesleyan holiness denominations. General superintendents G. B. Williamson and D. I. Vanderpool came to the Nazarenes from the Church of God (Holiness), a small and loosely-structured denomination that rigidly held to a congregational polity. The Nazarenes won over congregations from the Apostolic Holiness Union, the primary parent-body of the Pilgrim Holiness Church, including an influential church and school in Hutchinson, Kansas. That school evolved and by 1925 was known as Bresee College. Nazarenes were accused of "stealing sheep." Melvin E. Dieter, a church historian raised in the Pilgrim Holiness Church, put it diplomatically, saying that the Nazarenes "reaped where they did not sow." Charles Edwin Jones, another historian of the holiness movement, has offered an explanation for the Nazarene ability to attract people from other holiness denominations and their ability to grow larger than sister holiness churches. He asserts that the Nazarenes stood out from other holiness groups simply because they had a knack for organization.[2] Nazarenes founders took organization more seriously and developed it more highly than the Wesleyan Methodists, the Pilgrim Holiness, the Church of God (Holiness), and other closely-related groups of the early twentieth century.

Not every Nazarene has appreciated this knack. H. B. Hosley, an early district superintendent in the East, took his church in Washington, D.C., out of the denomination because of his disdain for the Church of the Nazarene's essentially Methodist structure. Another early Nazarene, Seth Rees, a former Quaker, rebelled against Nazarene organization and procedures repeatedly while a pastor on the Southern California District. The escalating tensions between Rees and district leaders created a sharp spirit of division on the district and threatened the very existence of Nazarene University in Pasadena (now Point Loma Nazarene University).

---

[2] Jones stated this view in a personal conversation with the author.

The resulting schism on the Southern California District roiled the entire denomination for a time. In the 1950s and 1960s, the Bible Missionary Church and the Church of the Bible Covenant originated with men and women who withdrew from the Nazarene fellowship in part because of what they (like Rees and Hosley before them) perceived as an excess of "ecclesiasticism."

Phineas Bresee was the person primarily responsible for the Nazarene system. After several years of loose organization, he began in 1904 using the Methodist Episcopal model (under which he had labored for thirty years) as the model for organizing the Nazarene movement on the West Coast. Methodist structure and procedures became embedded in the later Manuals for the western wing of the church. These, in turn, became the template for the Manual of the united church as it was constructed through mergers in 1907 and 1908. There was one primary modification that Nazarenes made to Methodist structure. Methodist structure has four levels: local, district, conference, and general. Nazarenes simplified the structure to three: local, district and general. In this simplified structure, the Nazarene district combined into a single unit the Methodist conference and district.

J. B. Chapman inducting G. B. Williamson into the office of general superintendent. In his induction address, Chapman stated his philosophy of the relationship of district and general superintendency to the Church of the Nazarene as a whole.

Like the Methodists, the Nazarenes traditionally maintained a close working relationship between the bishops (or general superintendents) and the district superintendents. J. B. Chapman explained this concept of interdependence when he inducted G. B. Williamson into the office of general superintendent in 1946. The setting was the chapel of Nazarene Theological Seminary in Kansas City, Missouri. In his induction address, Chapman noted that *superintendency* and *connectionalism* were intertwined. He said that the Church of the Nazarene "is a federation, not a confederation. The distinction is this … [T]he Church of the Nazarene is composed of ministers and members, not of churches and districts. … [S]uperintendency is of the whole church and all of the members of the church, and not simply of some sub-divisions or sections." Chapman emphasized two particular points: the general superintendents are "superintendents of the whole church, and not of some special area or section of the church. And the district superintendents are in reality assistant general superintendents, and not superintendents of independent units." Then he declared: "This conception is basic in our system."[3]

Chapman always chose his words very carefully. His distinction between a *federation* and a *confederation* was based on a well-known chapter in early American history. After the War of Independence, the thirteen former colonies became sovereign states that acted together for several years under a weak form of government called "The Articles of Confederation." The states retained their sovereignty in this confederation, but this form of government also proved to be impractical and failed to create a workable union; so a new government—*a federal government*—was established under a strong Constitution, and this time the states ceded much of their authority to the federal system. And here was Chapman's point: Nazarene districts and churches are units, but not independent units, and so the Church of the Nazarene is not a confederation of independent entities. Rather, it is a federation in which churches and districts are units within one connectional system. It is only on that basis that Chapman could say that "district superintendents are in reality assistant general superintendents" who assist general superintendents in their administration of "the whole church." *This* cluster of ideas is what Chapman insisted was "basic in our system."

A close working relationship existed between general and district superintendents throughout the church's first half-century. It was fundamental to Nazarene organization and life. The correspondence

---

[3] J. B. Chapman, "Induction Service for General Superintendent Williamson," typescript, J. B. Chapman Collection, Nazarene Archives, Lenexa, Kansas.

collections of H. F. Reynolds, John Goodwin, and R. T. Williams bear ample testimony to this. The H. F. Reynolds Collection at the Nazarene Archives contains over 24,000 pieces of correspondence, averaging three pieces of correspondence for every day that Reynolds was a general superintendent (1907 to 1932). As he traveled, Reynolds carried a portable typewriter, and in the mind's eye one can imagine him laying his coat across his knees, setting the typewriter across the coat, and banging out letters in the train coach, annoying his fellow passengers. His letters and those of his colleagues demonstrate the high degree to which general superintendents stayed in regular contact with district superintendents and even pastors. But there was much more. There was direct contact as well. Consider the role of district culture in the denomination's first half-century. District culture had two distinct centers: the annual camp meeting and the district assembly. The general superintendents were involved with both. The district camp meeting was a retreat that occurred in a rural area. It usually lasted a week. Each general superintendent spoke at several camp meetings a year, where they could be approached by clergy and laity alike. And there was the district assembly, which typically took five to seven days. The general superintendent was present for all of it. The district superintendent had the general superintendent's ear for that week, but so, too, did many pastors. Through frequent contact, Nazarene pastors and laity came to believe that they *knew personally* their general superintendents; they had spoken with them and taken their measure. Bonds of loyalty are formed through such shared activities and mutual communication.

This degree of intimacy was possible because the General Assembly steadily increased the size of the Board of General Superintendents throughout the church's first half-century. The board began with two members in 1907, expanded to three in 1908, to four in 1928, to five in 1952, and to six in 1960. At each point where the Board of General Superintendents was enlarged, the ratio of general superintendents to districts and district superintendents became more favorable. The ratio almost never exceeded 1:25 and typically stayed below 1:20.

And then something strange happened on the Nazarene road to the New Jerusalem. As the church outside Anglo-North America grew through the systematic planting of cross-cultural missions, the number of Nazarene districts expanded until there were 455 districts around the world before 2013. But the Board of General Superintendents did not correspondingly evolve; its membership has remained frozen at six for a half-century, and the consequences are striking.

The 1980 General Assembly adopted the policy of *internationalization* for the future Church of the Nazarene. By so doing, it affirmed the philosophy that Nazarenes would enter the future as one people in one church, rather than breaking up into national churches as earlier Protestant groups had done. As we discussed in chapter five, the decision to embrace internationalization swung on two hinges. The first was the mania for a *mission to the world* that characterized Nazarenes throughout their first century. The other hinge was new technology. The Church of the Nazarene had a democratic constitution, and a church with this system of governance requires participation and representation from all of its constituents. Until the twentieth century, earlier modes of transportation and communication made it impractical for Christians on different continents to be connected in meaningful ways. The twentieth century changed that. Routine airline travel, telephone and now e-mail communications—all the technological changes that have facilitated travel and communication—changed the mental horizons by the time Nazarenes had to decide their church's future. In 1980, internationalization seemed possible and was. And so that road was taken.

But the 1980 General Assembly took no steps to increase the number of general superintendents. And without a meaningful ratio of general superintendents to districts, an entirely new tier of bureaucracy was created and every Nazarene outside the United States and Canada was brought under its structure. The church created six world regions and put a regional director in charge of each. Even the United Kingdom was brought under this structure, though one of the early parent denominations originated there in 1906 and British missionaries were an integral part of the church's cross-cultural ministries for nearly a century. At the beginning of 2013, there were 80 districts in the United States and Canada and 375 districts in other parts of the world. And what has happened to Chapman's conception—the conception that he considered "fundamental"—that emphasizes a close working partnership between general and district superintendents, so much so that district superintendents are "in reality" assistant general superintendents? Simply put, it has been vitiated. Regional directors became the "assistant general superintendents" and added an insulating layer between the general superintendents and those district superintendents serving the church in Europe, Africa, Asia, Latin America, the Caribbean, and the Pacific nations. The new reality was, and is, not equitable. The district superintendents in Los Angeles, Indianapolis, and Atlanta can still pick up their phones and speak directly to their jurisdictional general superintendent much of the time. The district superintendents in Nairobi, New Delhi, and São Paulo cannot. The restricted size of the Board of General Superintendents in relation to the number of districts has created inequity; and it can be argued reasonably that maintaining this status quo constitutes a neo-colonial project.[4]

The perpetuation of a small Board of General Superintendents has prevented that body from growing diverse and representative of the various nationalities and life experiences that characterize the Nazarene people today. In 2013, only 30 percent of Nazarenes live in the United States, yet every member of the Board of General Superintendents, with two exceptions, have been American or Canadian.[5] Had the Board of General Superintendents grown proportionally with the expanding number of congregations and districts, there would have been more points of access to the church's highest elective office. In terms of representation on that board, key thresholds of gender, race, and world region likely would have been crossed long before they actually were. Moreover, district assemblies outside the United States and Canada are often stacked one after another, with the general superintendent moving from one assembly to another on consecutive days, staying long enough to preach, ordain ministers, and preside briefly. The regional director who travels with him or her gets the general superintendent's ear, but it is doubtful that pastors or even the district superintendents do so in any meaningful way. In recent General Assemblies there have been "repeater" resolutions—resolutions that crop up from one General Assembly to the next—that propose moving district assemblies to an every-other-year basis. The rationale has been that there are too many district assemblies for six general superintendents to attend. But the question must be raised: Isn't the basic problem with the number "six"? If the church has already been reengineered in some ways to accommodate a small Board of General Superintendents, and if attempts are made to reengineer it further for the same reason, then isn't the tail now wagging the ecclesiastical dog?[6]

---

[4] Statistics in this paragraph and the one following are based on: Office of the General Secretary, Church of the Nazarene, "The Church at Work: General Statistics by Region, 2012 Statistical Year."

[5] Eugenio Duarte, an African from Cape Verde, was elected to the Board of General Superintendents in 2009, and Gustavo Crocker, a Hispanic from Guatemala, was elected in 2013.

[6] Also see Bill Sullivan, et al, "Shall We Reinvent Our 100 Year Old Denomination? Surveying Organizational Models," a paper discussed at the 2005 meeting of the Association of Nazarene Sociologists and Researchers, available through the ANSR website. Sullivan and co-contributors state that an essential characteristic of a revitalized church includes "the multiplication of leaders at all levels of the church," and warns that failure to multiply at any level will create a bottle-neck, and "the organization will be negatively affected." http://www.nazarene.org/files/docs/OrganizationalModel.pdf.

A quarter-century ago, historian Paul Bassett predicted that any future schisms in the Church of the Nazarene would be different from those of the 1950s and 1960s, when theology and life-style issues were at the heart of agitation within Nazarene circles. He predicted, instead, that future schisms would be geographical in nature and based on an inability to accommodate cultural differences and work out equitable systems of governance. Essentially, he predicted, it would be difficult for Americans to share leadership in a growing global church.

There are compelling issues involved. Should the church move further away from modes of governance and deeper into management modes? Will leaders keep reengineering the church to accommodate a small Board of General Superintendents, or will the church undertake a mid-course correction that, no matter how wrenching initially, will return us to Chapman's fundamental conception? Or is Chapman's "fundamental conception" simply an artifact, outdated and no longer viable? Let's put a finer point on this. Should policy for a group of contiguous districts, such as the districts of southern Africa, be made within a system of management, or should it be made by the district superintendents meeting together under the leadership of a general superintendent who knows them? The first method is the American CEO model. The second is Chapman's model. The church has choices to make. It can simply continue as it has done and hope that nothing breaks. Or it can expand the Board of General Superintendents to create favorable ratios of general leaders to district leaders and return to Chapman's "fundamental conception" that characterized the denomination until the 1970s. Or it can move in the precise opposite direction, rejecting governance mode in favor of management mode, and making permanent the layer of insulation between general and district superintendents.

Which way will the Church of the Nazarene go? There is no telling which path it will take, but one thing is perfectly clear: these issues have grown out of our past and are the product of a lengthy process of historical development. History is setting our table.

THE AMERICAN CHURCH AND THE INTERNATIONAL CHURCH

There is another issue that arises directly out of our past. In recent years, it is customary to hear jeremiads regarding the low growth rate of the American branch of the Church of the Nazarene. Church leaders often voice this concern. Sometimes this concern is coupled by contrasting it with the higher growth rate among Nazarenes in other world areas. When such comparisons are made, the implication seems to be that American

Nazarenes are not doing well, that they are losing religious fervor and need to pray for revival, and that their commitment is fading. Pastors sometimes feel that the message from church leaders is that they are failing. Often enough, someone trots out the old canard that "denominations tend to cool down when they reach 100." The implication is that the denomination, at least in North America, is ailing at its centennial. Here is an instance where a firmer grasp of history can help us understand the present and better anticipate the church's future.

First, let's strike down the myth that religious organizations tend to falter as they reach their 100-year mark. Whoever put this bit of "wisdom" out into the religious consciousness did not know what they were talking about. American Presbyterians prospered in their first century and prospered even more in their second one. American Baptists and Methodists both had a great first century, but they both did even better in their second century. There are many other examples.[7]

Religion always operates in a distinct social context, and American Christianity operates in a fundamentally different context from that of the Christian church in any other part of the world. The Church of the Nazarene originated in a time when all American churches were growing and church affiliation among Americans was on a slow but steady upswing. The early Nazarenes were the undeniable beneficiaries of that fact.

No one knows, for sure, what percentage of Americans were churched when the Republic was founded. Estimates have varied widely, from as low as 5 percent to as high as 20 percent. The actual percentage was probably somewhere between 10 and 15 percent. This fact surprises some people, since a ruling assumption among evangelicals and others is that America originated as a Christian nation and has consistently maintained a commitment to being "one nation under God" until the twentieth century, when secular trends began eroding America's fidelity to the churches.

And yet no picture could be further from the truth. In the 1980s, historian Jon Butler showed that the religion of the American colonists was a stew of religious beliefs, only some of which were drawn from Christian orthodoxy. Colonists also drew their religious beliefs from the magical world system, the occult, and witchcraft. Christian orthodoxy played a prominent role in colonial America to be sure, but this was because Christian orthodoxy, especially Calvinist orthodoxy, was particularly strong among the educated classes, who were more likely to be church members and more conventional and orthodox in their belief system than illiterate Americans. Thus orthodoxy cast a long shadow over American

---

[7] See, for instance, Figure 2 of Sullivan, et al.

thought and created a canopy that spread over American culture, but under that canopy the religious stew was much different.[8]

The remarkable detachment of Americans toward the churches and toward the Christian faith actually supplied early American churches with their primary mission. That mission was to win the allegiance of the American people, who often lost their religious moorings after they were no longer connected with the parish system of the Old World churches. American clergy set about this task of evangelism with great energy. Episcopalians, Lutherans, Congregationalists and Presbyterians all geared themselves toward that objective, but the Baptists and Methodists equipped themselves better and approached the task with more fervor.[9] All of these denominations created a department of home missions to plant churches, evangelize, and civilize the American people. The American Bible Society, whose survey showed that only a fraction of American families actually owned a Bible, formed in 1816 with the goal of placing a Bible in every American home. By 1850, the Methodists, which had only a few hundred members at the time of the American Revolution, were America's largest denomination, a status they maintained until immigration from central and Eastern Europe pushed the Roman Catholic Church ahead. Even then, Methodists remained the largest Protestant group until the mid-1920s, when Baptists finally overtook them. The slow upward curve of religious affiliation by 1850 led to the churching of about one third of Americans. By 1900, that fraction had climbed to about one half. Still, another two-thirds century passed until the percentage of churched Americans reached about 66 percent in the late 1960s. After that, church affiliation dipped for several years, only to climb upward again and maintain itself in the 60 percent range or higher ever since. The effort to evangelize Americans and win them to the churches took over 175 years if we date its beginning from the early Republic, or over 200 years if we date it from the Great Awakening. Two-thirds of that span had elapsed when the Nazarenes stepped onto the scene, and Nazarene growth in America is tied to that trend, as are the growth stories of other denominations, including the Pentecostals who emerged in the same period. Similarly,

---

[8] See Jon Butler, *Awash on a Sea of Faith* (Cambridge, Mass.: Harvard University Press, 1990). For instance, while church attendance was quite high during New England's earliest decades, it declined sharply afterwards, and only 17 percent of residents of Salem, Mass., were church members by 1683.

[9] Franklin H. Littell's study, *From State Church to Pluralism* (New York: The Macmillan Company, 1962) interpreted the grand sweep of American religious history in light of this phenomenon. He asserted that the evangelization of a pagan American people more closely resembled the evangelization of pagan Europe in the early Middle Ages, rather than the mythic "Christian America" of modern imagination.

when church affiliation peaked, all denominations found it more difficult to grow, including evangelical ones.[10]

The United States is the third most populous nation in the world and yet it sustains the highest rate of church attendance of nearly any nation in the world. With the presence of multitudes of churches and decades of Christian radio and television broadcasts, American society is saturated with Christian messages. To put it in market terms, a saturated market is a tough market in which to grow.

What does this mean for the future of Nazarenes? First, our pastors are not failing. Nazarenes have held their place in the religious economy. They are not losing members as some denominations are doing, and while an annual growth rate of a fraction of a percent is not exciting, it should not be discouraging. Remember that it took over 175 years to move American church affiliation from under 20 percent up to 66 percent. That long uphill climb averaged just slightly better than one-fourth of one percent gain per year—and this was during the heyday of American church growth. American Nazarenes actually do better than that, and they do so with an American society in which many other denominations are moving in the other direction.

Nazarene growth outside the United States is also part of a wider story. The central theme of Africa's twentieth century religious history is the conversion of its peoples from traditional polytheistic religions to monotheistic faiths—Christianity and Islam, with each major faith now embracing over 40 percent of Africans. In 1900 only 1.6 percent of the world's Christians lived in Africa. Today, nearly one in five Christians lives there, as the number of African Christians rose from nearly 8.8 million in 1900 to over 420 million today. The Church of the Nazarene has fared quite well within the context of African evangelization. For nearly 80 years, the Nazarene presence in Africa was concentrated in the South—Swaziland, South Africa, Mozambique, and Angola. In the 1970s and 1980s, the church's movement into East Africa and West Africa expanded its boundaries significantly and met with considerable success. The establishment of Africa Nazarene University in Nairobi in the 1980s was an important milestone in that development. This expansion continues. One notable example is in Ethiopia, where an East African revival has driven impressive Protestant growth, not only among Nazarenes but also among Assemblies of God and the Meserete Kristos Church—the church that Mennonite missionaries left behind when the Marxist government

---

[10] Roger Finke and Rodney Stark, *The Churching of America, 1776–1990* (New Brunswick, N.J.: 1992), esp. Ch. 1.

came to power in the 1970s. Under Ethiopian leadership, the Meserete Kristos has become the largest Mennonite denomination in the world. In many ways, the growth of African Christianity in the twentieth century has parallels with the growth of American Christianity from 1765 to 1965. Nazarenes have been full participants in the Ethiopian revival. Churches, members, and districts have multiplied in recent years. Nazarene growth across Africa has taken the denomination from just over 41,000 members in 1984 to over 457,000 today. Twenty-four percent of Nazarenes are now Africans. Their surging numbers are changing the denomination. At the same time, their story is part of a wider story of world evangelization.[11]

In Asia the number of Christians soared from under 21 million in 1900 to 355 million by 2008, while the *Protestantization* of Latin American religion is a phenomenon that spurs the growth of evangelical churches there. As much as Africans, the Asian and Latin American Nazarenes have very distinct growth stories of their own. And like the Africans and Americans, the Church of the Nazarene's story of expansion in these areas is not an isolated occurrence but part of a much wider Christian story.

What Paradigm for the Twenty-First Century?

In many ways, the Church of the Nazarene's first century was the projection of lengthened shadows cast by two early leaders: Phineas Bresee and Hiram F. Reynolds. Both contributed distinctive elements to Nazarene life, and their visions of the church have resonated ever since.

As we saw in previous chapters, their visions were not identical. Those visions connected at various places but were not the same. Bresee's distinctive contribution was to the church's frame of government, a democratic form of American Methodism. But this form of government was merely instrumental. It was not the reason for the church or the purpose behind it; it was only the structure that held it together and gave it coherence. Instead, Bresee said repeatedly that the purpose behind the Church of the Nazarene was to "Christianize Christianity."

The phrase was not original with him. It was commonly used in the Social Gospel literature of the early twentieth century, and it became more widely known after Walter Rauschenbusch published *Christianity and the Social Crisis* and *Christianizing the Social Order*. There is no evidence

---

[11] David B. Barrett, Todd M. Johnson, and Peter F. Crossing, "Missiometrics 2008: Reality Checks for Christian World Communions," *International Bulletin of Missionary Research*, Vol. 32, No. 1 (January 2008): 30. And "The Church at Work: 1985 General Statistics, Church of the Nazarene," *Herald of Holiness* (Jan. 1, 1986): 22–23; and "The Church at Work: General Statistics, September 30, 2009," circulated by the Office of the General Secretary, Church of the Nazarene.

that Bresee read social gospel literature, and his use of the term was not the same except in one sense: like the social gospel theologians, Bresee regarded the present state of Christendom as deficient, lying below the plane that it loftily claimed to occupy. For Rauschenbusch and the social gospel theologians, the deficiency in Christendom lay in its unwillingness to critique the harsh realities of industrial capitalism and its effects on working men and women. They saw exploitation in the alliance between big capital and compliant religion, with injustice and abuse as the dark underside of this reality. Bresee's critique of Christendom did not engage in an analysis of industrial culture but focused on the perceived gap between having "a form of religion" and "denying the power thereof." Bresee looked at the poor and saw people who needed a pastor. He looked at the urban situation and saw a need for family-oriented churches among the poor. "Christianizing Christianity" was, for him, a multi-faceted program that emphasized creating centers of "holy fire" in America's urban centers. These centers of holy fire were to be sustained by revival but they were not to exist just to be emotional baths. Bresee emphasized an essential integrity between vital religious experience and ministry to the poor. His associates went out and developed ministries among the Mexican, Chinese, and Japanese populations in Southern California. "Christianizing Christianity" was about linking revival and social renewal, about urban ministry and multicultural ministry. It was about maintaining the tie between a profession of entire sanctification and the sanctified life.

He was a true Wesleyan on this point. Wesley had insisted on the "witness of the Spirit" to God's converting and sanctifying grace. The witness was both inner and outer. The inner witness was one's calm assurance that God had performed a work of grace in his or her life. The outer witness was a witness that others could see. It was manifested powerfully in the fruits of the Spirit enumerated by St. Paul, but it was also manifested through fidelity to the standards of Jesus Christ in Matthew 25 ("For I was hungry, and you fed me; I was thirsty, and you gave me drink; I was a stranger, and you took me in; Naked, and you clothed me; I was sick, and you visited me; I was in prison, and you came to me.") and Luke 4:18–19 ("The Spirit of the Lord is with me. He has anointed me to tell the Good News to the poor. He has sent me to announce forgiveness to the prisoners of sin and the restoring of sight to the blind, to forgive those who have been shattered by sin, to announce the year of the Lord's favor.").

We noted in chapter one that early British Methodism became a world movement because the Wesleys took their societies to the poor. Bresee understood this. Like B. T. Roberts, the Free Methodist founder, and William and Catherine Booth, the Salvation Army founders, he stood in a train of Wesleyan holiness leaders who found integrity in the union of vital religious experience and ministry to the social outsiders. It was a unified view. Religious revival was its heartbeat; concrete ministry "to the least of these" was its practical outworking. "Christianizing Christianity" was about narrowing "the holiness credibility gap," as Mildred Wynkoop later called it. It was about a profession of holiness matched by a life of holiness; about understanding that "talk about holiness" is premature unless it links to new social realities that can grow only from the hearts and lives of people who take seriously reconciliation with God. It was about a holy church at work among the people, calling and leading them to repentance, reformation, sanctification, and integration.

The vision of H. F. Reynolds was different. He did not disagree with Bresee's vision, but his passion lay elsewhere—in evangelizing the world. Reynolds played the key role in stamping the Church of the Nazarene with a mission-minded mentality, and his paradigm of a mission to the world became an integrating vision that helped unite the disparate groups that came together between 1907 and 1915, gathering them around a common vision. It is fair to say that Reynolds' paradigm emerged as the central paradigm out of which the Church of the Nazarene lived its first century. It was the paradigm out of which *internationalization* later emerged. It led to transformed lives and a transformed church.

The mission to the world as an exercise in cross-cultural missions will continue to shape Nazarenes life for a while yet—perhaps another thirty or forty years. But to even contemplate the end of the cross-cultural mission as we have known it is to raise the next question: What happens then? When the Nazarenes are organized in all nations of Earth, when the era of mission expansion is over, will we still have a *raison d'etre*? What does the end of "the mission to the world" as Nazarenes have known it for over a century mean to the Nazarene psyche and sense of self-identity?

John Venn, the venerable priest of Clapham parish, told the first Anglican missionaries to India that their job was not to introduce the people of India to Christianity. The Indians had lived with English colonial rulers for a century and had already formed an opinion of Christianity. No, Venn said, the missionaries' task was to help Indians perceive the difference between "the nominal Christian" who had exploited them from the *real* Christian, whose passion is the Kingdom of God and its righteousness. Over the past two decades, we have witnessed European Christians massacring Moslems in Bosnia and Kosovo. The horrendous massacres in Rwanda occurred in a nation that was considered to be the most Roman Catholic nation in Africa.

As we survey a divided and troubled Christendom, is it not appropriate to ask, once again, how to blend Bresee's agenda of "Christianizing Christianity" with our mission to the world? Will Bresee's paradigm become more necessary than ever before, since it concerns the church's integrity as it proclaims the Gospel through word and deed?

Nazarenes and the Christian Economy

Our history brings one more issue to the fore: How should Nazarenes see themselves in the world Christian economy of the twenty-first century? As an international church, Nazarenes have created a distinctive footprint in the world.

Nazarenes were reluctant to enter into partnership with other denominations during their first half-century. Lewis T. Corlett led Nazarene observers who attended the organizing convention of the National Association of Evangelicals in 1942, but church leaders took no action to join that organization. It wasn't until 1969 that the church joined the Christian Holiness Association, the direct lineal descendent of the National Camp Meeting Association for the Promotion of Holiness that had spawned the Church of the Nazarene. Nazarenes then joined the National Association of Evangelicals in 1984. These were the church's only affiliations for the next 25 years. These were American organizations, and Nazarene participation reflected the denomination's predominantly American ethos at that time. One of the most important steps at the end of the twentieth century was joining the World Methodist Council in 1999. For the first time since embracing *internationalization*, Nazarenes established a relationship with an interchurch body whose footprint actually resembled their own. In so doing, Nazarenes joined the Wesleyan Church, the Free Methodist Church of Canada, and the Free Methodist Church of North America—the denominations most closely associated with their doctrine, life, and history—in participating in this organization of the world Methodist family. Since then, the church has established another affiliation as a voting member of the European Methodist Council—a step fostered by Rev. Thomas Vollenveider, former superintendent of the Northeast German District, and recommended by the Eurasia Regional Office.

I want to complete this circle by revisiting the basic trajectory of Nazarene history. That trajectory can be described by cribbing a phrase from the spiritual writer Elizabeth O'Connor. It has been both a journey inward and a journey outward, and each journey has involved two dimensions.

The first dimension is that of organizational structure and geographic expansion. The journey inward in terms of organizational structure lies in the movement to overcome the sectarian divisions in the holiness movement by uniting into one, strong holiness denomination. Mergers were the means through which this unity was sought and achieved. From the many came one. The outward aspect of this dimension was the mission to the world that gave the Nazarenes an international presence, which then was consolidated as an international church. From the one came many—a church of diverse tongues and cultures whose very being reflects the great truth that "God invites to His church those of all ages, races, and nations."

The second dimension lies in the inner history of the Nazarene psyche. At this level, the inward journey was a journey into insularity that came about by erecting a sectarian shield that separated Nazarenes not only from culture but also from other Christians who were different in belief and behavior. The sectarian shield was intimately related to specific concepts of holiness, but it was due even more to the growth of premillenialism among Nazarenes. Premillenialism's emphasis on "the fallenness" and presumed apostasy of the Christian churches at large became deeply embedded in the Nazarene psyche and essentially robbed Nazarenes of any meaningful degree of ecumenical soul. The sectarian shield not only preserved Nazarenes from unholy influences but from participation and fellow-feeling with other Christians, except those who closely resembled us in worship and ethos. But the Nazarene psyche has also experienced an outward journey that proceeds slowly but steadily, not toward compromise with the world but toward new engagement and witness. The Wesleyan Theological Society became an avenue through which Nazarene scholars participated in creating a community of Wesleyan scholars across denominational lines. A further development is the participation of Nazarene scholars in the Oxford Institute of Methodist Theological Studies, an involvement which dates back to at least the mid-1970s. Nazarene participation in the Christian Holiness Association, then the National Association of Evangelicals, and now the World Methodist Council and the European Methodist Council represent further steps away from isolation and into participation in the wider church.

In 1995, Carl Bangs published a paper in the *Historical Bulletin* of the World Methodist Historical Society. It was titled "John Wesley, P. F. Bresee, and the Church Universal," and it was initially created and read to a group of Nazarene pastors at Nazarene Theological Seminary. After surveying the various ways in which Wesley and Bresee both affirmed the universal church of God, Bangs noted that when the Church of the Nazarene ordains ministers, they are not ordained as ministers in the Church of the Nazarene but as ministers "in the Church of God." That phrase is used by the presiding general superintendent and printed on the ordination certificate. Bangs concluded: Nazarene pastors are ministers in a wide church, not a narrow one, and they should be aware of that fact.[12]

By the very same token, general superintendents are elected to oversee the congregations and interests of the Church of the Nazarene, but they, too, are bishops in a wide church. And the Nazarene people, who are baptized as Christians, not as Nazarenes, are likewise members in a wide church. The crumbling of the sectarian shield that once defined Nazarenes should mean the rediscovery of Christian identity, not its loss, as we confront the issues thrust upon us by our past.

---

[12] *Historical Bulletin of the World Methodist Historical Society*, Vol. 24 (Third Quarter 1995): 3–6.

www.ingramcontent.com/pod-product-compliance
Lightning Source LLC
Chambersburg PA
CBHW070920180426
43192CB00038B/2049